Puppy Training Combo

Contains

Housetraining Success Formula
6 Simple Steps to Housetraining Your Puppy or Dog

&

Puppy Training
Six Weeks to a Better-Behaved Puppy

By

Carol Miller

Liability Disclaimer

By reading this document, you assume all risks associated with using the advice given below, with a full understanding that you, solely, are responsible for anything that may occur as a result of putting this information into action in any way, and regardless of your interpretation of the advice.

This book is intended for educational purposes only and does not replace a consultation with a certified animal behaviorist, veterinarian, or other qualified animal professional.

From the Author

This bargain book combo is a compilation of two of my best-selling dog training books for puppies. Each book is presented here in full, along with the included bonuses. With this information, you have what you need to get your puppy off to a great start!

I wish you the best in training your puppy!

Carol Miller

www.ReallySimpleDogTraining.com

Table of Contents

Housetraining Success Formula

6 Simple Steps to Housetraining Your Puppy or Dog

A "Really Simple Dog Training" Booklet

By: Carol Miller, CDT

INTRODUCTION

Welcome to "Housetraining Success Formula: 6 Simple Steps to Housetraining Your Puppy or Dog," part of the *Really Simple Dog Training* series of short, easy-to-follow booklets on how to turn your puppy or dog into a great pet! You won't find a lot of fluff here, just simple real-life information.

If you're reading this, it's pretty safe to assume that you have a dog that needs to be housetrained. Maybe you've had other dogs that you've housetrained without problems and for some reason this one is not getting it, or it could be that this is your first time owning a dog, and you need some help. Let me say up front that housetraining a puppy or dog is simple – not necessarily easy – if you follow the program outlined here. It would be great to promise that the job is easy and effortless, but then I would have to have a magic wand that I could wave over a puppy and POOF! he's housetrained. As much as I would love to be able to perform miracles, I, like you, must rely on proven, simple training principles to help my puppy become a great pet. NOTE: I will be using the word puppy from now on, but the same methods apply to older dogs as well.

Before we get down to it, it's important to understand some basics about dog training – positive reinforcement dog training, to be specific. This type of training is based on scientifically proven techniques that work *without punishment*. I want to be clear here – **punishment has no place in housetraining**. I'll explain exactly how it can actually work against your goal – a reliably housetrained puppy – in just a bit, but for now, please treat those old-fashioned ideas of training, such as rubbing the puppy's nose in it, hitting him with a newspaper, shaking him, etc.

as what they are – old ideas that never worked well and will actually damage your relationship with your puppy. The good news is that you can train your puppy in ways that help him feel safe and secure while quickly learning what you want him to do.

HOW YOUR PUPPY SEES THE WORLD

So many times dog owners say, "I just want a good dog!" The joke's on them – they already have one! If your dog pees and poops in the house, chews your furniture, jumps on your guests, barks at everything that moves, drags you down the street during walks, and won't come when you call, he's just being a dog, the way dogs are born to act. Your puppy wasn't born knowing that carpets are expensive and he should respect that – he thinks, "What a nice absorbent surface, perfect for peeing!" Everything is a chew toy for a puppy, and life is meant to be fun, which translates into tons of unwanted behaviors. We love dogs, but we don't love "natural" dogs; rather, we love well-trained pet dogs. Since what we want from puppies is totally unnatural for them, it's our responsibility to patiently educate them as to how we would like them to behave, keeping in mind just how unnatural that is. Frankly, I find it amazing how good-natured most dogs are about changing to fit our lifestyle!

BASIC TRAINING CONCEPT: PREVENTION

The absolutely most important thing to keep in mind in changing any unwanted behavior in an animal is to prevent it from happening in the first place. In this booklet we are addressing your puppy having accidents in the house. The unwanted behavior is peeing and/or pooping in the house. So the most important thing to do to change this is to make sure when humanly possible that it never happens. "Oh," I hear you say, "but it does happen, all the time, and I can't prevent it." Well read on, and I will show you how you can, through proper management and attention.

To understand the importance of this, try to see it as if you are working on breaking a bad habit of your own. Every time you do that thing, you are strengthening the habit, making it even harder to break. This is what happens in housetraining. Every time the puppy has an accident in the house, he feels more comfortable doing it next time. You need to build the understanding in him that OUTSIDE is the place to go, by repeated successes, without him building the habit of going indoors.

BASIC TRAINING CONCEPT: IGNORE ACCIDENTS

Okay, I admit it – no one can prevent accidents one hundred percent of the time. So what do you do if one gets by you? You clean it up, period. No scolding, no punishment, no acknowledgement that it even happened. Simply smack yourself with a newspaper and determine that it won't happen again. I'll be discussing proper clean-up later.

BASIC TRAINING CONCEPT: REWARD SUCCESSES

Science has shown us that when behavior is rewarded, it is likely to be repeated. If you want to see your puppy do his business outside more often, then you'd better reward him when he goes in his potty place. This means that until he is reliably trained, you must not just let him out the door – if you aren't with him, you can't reward him. I'll be going into the reward process in depth shortly.

BEFORE WE START

How Long Can He Hold His Bladder?

It's important to understand that young puppies and small dogs cannot hold their bladder for extended periods of time, so you must take this into consideration when house-training. The general guideline is at MOST, his age in months plus one. This means that a three month old puppy *might* be able to hold his bladder for 4 hours. But this is an estimate (consider yourself – can you hold your own bladder reliably every day for the same amount of time? I know I can't). In addition, if the puppy is sleeping or lying down quietly, he can hold it much longer than if he is running around.

How Long Will It Take To Housetrain My Puppy?

As with most things in life, this will depend primarily on how committed you are to the process. If you are diligent, you will see much faster results than if you put in a half-hearted effort. Older puppies are capable of being fully housetrained faster than young pups, since they are more physically and emotionally mature. It may just take a few weeks, and it may take months, but you will see improvements if you are following the program described here. My advice is that it will take how long it takes – if you set a mental deadline, you are more likely to become frustrated, which will work against you.

What If I Can't Be Home During The Day?

I have included a section that addresses this in Appendix A: Troubleshooting.

Can I Paper Train or Litter Train My Puppy?

A brief discussion of this can be found in Appendix A: Troubleshooting. Keep in mind that it becomes much more difficult to train a puppy to go outside once you have taught that it is okay to use a place inside.

THE SUCCESS FORMULA

STEP 1: MANAGEMENT

The most important step in housetraining is to manage your puppy so there are as few mistakes as possible, and of course, none is best. This won't mean he is housetrained at first, just that you have taken steps to see to it that he doesn't need to go in the house by keeping him confined to a small area he won't want to soil, getting him outside so that he can relieve himself there, and during playtime you never take your eyes off of him.

CONFINEMENT

This step is crucial – a normal puppy will not want to soil his bed, so the space he has when not supervised must be small enough for him to comfortably lie down and turn around, but not so large that he can soil the corner and still sleep away from it. Ordinarily this is a crate, either a wire dog cage or a plastic "airline carrier" style crate. For a puppy who is likely to grow a lot, there are crates that have a divider in them that can be moved as he gets larger. Another alternative is a small exercise pen, or X-Pen, but it must not have too much space in it.

Your puppy must be in this area unless he is with someone who is actively watching him. This doesn't mean playing with your kids – they are much too likely to forget about the puppy while watching TV or playing video games. Unless you have an unusually responsible child, this should be the job of an adult. Remember, no accidents is your goal, so keeping the puppy loose in a room with someone who isn't thinking about him will set you back.

Your puppy's crate should be a stress-free resting spot for him, one that he learns to love. It's best to put a treat in with him every single time you crate him – this will help him to like going in. Also, if you put him in with a kong toy with a bit of cheese whiz or peanut butter smeared in it, he will have something to do, and will settle down easier. For dozens of ideas on creative ways to stuff a kong, just do an internet search for "kong recipes".

It's a good idea to have the crate in the bedroom with you at night so that you can hear if he needs to go out. In the "Troubleshooting" section in Appendix A, I discuss how to keep your puppy from waking you just to have some fun in the middle of the night.

KEY POINT: Crate your puppy unless you are watching him like a hawk.

STEP 2: SCHEDULE

SCHEDULE HIS MEALS

If your puppy is eating on a schedule, it will be much easier for you to judge when he will need to eliminate. Young puppies should eat four times a day, older puppies three times, and adult dogs twice. Consult your vet about the correct eating schedule for your puppy. Be sure he has access to water whenever he is out of his crate, but do not put water in the crate itself. Also, take up his water bowl after 7pm. If he runs around and gets thirsty later than that, just allow him a short drink.

POTTY TIME, PLAYTIME, POTTY TIME, REST TIME, REPEAT…

The closer you can keep to a schedule of rest/playtimes, the easier it will be to train your pup. Here's a typical schedule for an untrained puppy:

First thing in the morning, put puppy on leash, take puppy immediately to potty area, wait for puppy to pee, reward, bring in for breakfast. Have 15 minutes of supervised playtime, and take back out to potty area for poop. If he doesn't eliminate in 5 minutes or so, bring him in and crate him for 15 minutes. Then take him out again. Repeat this until he has eliminated. At this point he can have supervised playtime, but should go outside to pee every 15 minutes or so if he is running around, no more than 30 minutes if he is calmly chewing a toy or just playing quietly. After a total of 30 minutes or so of playtime, take him out to potty, and then put him in the crate for two hours or so. Then bring him out to his potty spot. If he pees, reward and take him for a walk or bring him in for some playtime, about 30 minutes with a potty break in the middle. Then see if he'll potty again before crating him. Repeat this process all day, 2 hours in the crate, 30 minutes out of the crate, with potty trips every 15 minutes while not crated, being sure to take a potty trip immediately after getting out of the crate and just before going in. He should not stay out of the crate unless he has peed during his potty trip. Also, he should go to his potty spot for a poop within 15 minutes of eating a meal. If he doesn't poop, return him to his crate for 15 minutes, as described above for breakfast. Don't give him playtime until he has pooped outside.

Late in the evening, go potty one last time, and put him to bed in his crate in your room. If he needs to go out during the night, quietly get up and take him out to his potty spot. Do not talk to him or engage him in any way that he might find fun, just wait for him to go potty, reward and quietly put him back to bed. Soon he should sleep through the night provided you don't let his night potty trips become fun time.

You may find it easier to keep to your 15 minute scheduled potty times by setting a timer or alarm – it's very easy to forget how long it's been.

Remember:

1 – Use the same spot every time.

2 – Take the puppy out on a leash.

3 – No playtime unless he's empty.

4 – Go out for a bowel movement within 15 minutes of a meal.

5 – Take him out to pee as soon as he comes out of the crate, every 15 minutes during supervised time, and before you crate him again.

6 – If he doesn't go within 5 minutes, then crate him for 15 minutes before trying again.

KEY POINT: The more you keep to a schedule, the faster you will see results.

STEP 3: SUPERVISION

I mentioned this in Step 1, but it's so important that I need to discuss it here as its own step. When your puppy is active, he will need to potty more often, sometimes as soon as 15 minutes for a young or small breed puppy. When he has his playtime, you must actively play with him or be watching him, or he may quickly have an accident. Yes, he may go right in front of you so fast you can't stop it, but most of the time if you are watching, you can get him out in time. Since he needs attention and time with you during his playtime, needing to keep a close eye on him helps to remind you to bond with him through play and other types of interaction.

While you are watching him closely, you should begin to see the signs that he has to go – sniffing, circling – and then you can rush him out to his potty spot. When you can recognize the signs, you are well on your way to getting him housetrained.

While he's out of the crate, it's best to keep him in one small room to help keep him from slipping out of sight into another area of the house. Close doors or use baby gates or furniture to block exits. If he spends his free time in the same room all the time, your puppy will begin to see it as his larger den, and this will reduce the chances of an accident here as well. Gradually move to other rooms as he seems to be able to handle it.

If you want your puppy free a bit more, you can consider hooking his leash to your belt so that he can't run off and get into trouble (this is good for preventing unwanted chewing as well). But you still are responsible for noticing if he starts acting like he needs to go outside. If you try this and find him going potty in the house next to you, you are probably using the leash as a substitute for watching him, which won't work.

KEY POINT: When he's loose, keep him with you in one room and watch him like a hawk.

STEP 4: WHEN HE DOES IT RIGHT

Okay, you have picked a potty spot, and you've leashed your puppy and taken him out to it. Now your job is to be boring. Simply stand still and let the puppy sniff around, but don't let him drag you with him. Just give him a bit of leash to move about, but you stand still and silent. This is NOT playtime. When he begins to look like he will go potty (or just starts), say "Go Potty" as he does his business, and as soon as he finishes, say "YES!" and give him a small, extra yummy treat and praise him as if he is the best puppy in the world. Then you can play with him or go for a walk or take him inside, according to your schedule. Remember you must always go with the puppy, or you won't be there to reward him. He won't connect what it's for if you don't give him his treat within one second of doing the right thing. And if you aren't with him, you won't be sure if he went, which means you can't be sure he's empty for playtime. So no exceptions – go with him leashed to his potty spot every time.

Treats for going potty should be better than anything he gets inside – small pieces of real meat or cheese, or a particularly delicious dog treat. You are doing a couple of things here: a) he is learning that when he goes outside, he gets an extra great treat and attention for going outside, which makes going outside much better than going inside, and b) you are actually beginning to teach him to go potty on command, which is wonderful later when you need him to go when you are in a hurry.

When he is fully housetrained, you won't need to feed him anymore for going potty – the relief he gets from the action will be reward enough – but for now, you want to really show him what a good idea it is to go in his spot.

KEY POINT: Always use the same potty spot, and take your puppy there on leash. Give a great treat and lots of attention when he goes in his potty spot.

STEP 5: WHEN HE DOES IT WRONG

Just as you are rewarding with treats and ATTENTION for doing the right thing, you must not give any attention to the puppy for making a mistake. Simply clean it up thoroughly. Use an enzymatic cleaner (they sell these at any pet store) in order to be sure the odor is neutralized. Even though you may not be able to smell it anymore, your dog might. Don't use ammonia to clean up a mess – it reminds your puppy of urine.

If you happen to catch your puppy in the act, you can try making a noise to interrupt him. If he stops in the middle, grab him and hurry to your potty spot to let him finish. Just make sure you don't make a noise that is so loud that you frighten him – this is NOT a punishment, just a distraction.

Never punish your puppy for a mistake. Period. He simply will not understand what you are punishing him for, and you run the risk of making him afraid to relieve himself in front of you. This will cause him to try to sneak out of sight so that he can relieve himself in the house when you aren't nearby, or to refuse to go while outside on the leash because he has learned that you may punish him when he eliminates. Don't ruin your puppy's trust in you by scaring or hurting him during his training.

Your goal is to get the puppy to understand that there is a difference between going potty inside the house and outside, and that going outside is MUCH better. And by practicing good management and supervision, you are establishing the habit of going outside and preventing the habit of going inside. Can you see how it all works together to help your puppy figure it out?

KEY POINT: Don't punish for mistakes – he just won't understand. Clean it up and move on.

STEP 6: KEEPING TRACK OF HOW HE'S DOING

This is something that most people don't bother with, but it can really help you succeed in your training. Print out a schedule sheet for each day, and mark on it when you went out, when the puppy ate, playtime, naptime, and when and where he peed and pooped. Highlight accidents, and look for trends. You may find that he always has an accident in the evening during playtime, so you can make a point of getting him out before it happens from now on. Also check to see if accidents are happening in a specific place or when a particular person is watching the puppy. This helps you figure ways to prevent it happening in the future.

There are three benefits to keeping track of what happens each day: first, it helps you to remember to follow your schedule; second as mentioned above, it helps you to notice trouble areas; and third, down the road when you feel that you aren't making any progress, you can pull out your early sheets and see how much better you are actually doing.

I have created a simple record-keeping page that I am happy to share with you, to thank you for purchasing this booklet. Just go to

www.ReallySimpleDogTraining.com/HSFBonus.html

and claim it.

KEY POINT: Record keeping is a great way to check on your progress and keep you on track.

SUMMARY

Step 1 – Manage your puppy's unsupervised time so he cannot have an accident by confining him to a crate or other small area.

Step 2 – Follow a strict schedule of rest, play and potty times. Remember that your puppy will need to go potty as frequently every 15 minutes while he is actively running around. Schedule his meals to help predict when he will have to have a bowel movement.

Step 3 – Supervise at all times when your puppy is not safely confined. This means your eyes must be on the puppy every second. Confine him to a single small room to make it easier for you to be sure he can't get out of sight. Move to other rooms as he shows he is doing well. Pay attention to his signals that he is about to relieve himself and hurry him out to his potty spot before he can have an accident.

Step 4 – REWARD with food and attention when your puppy eliminates outside. Be sure he learns that going outside means it's a party! Be sure to teach him to hurry and go by having play and/or a walk AFTER he goes. Remember to take him to the same spot each time to help him understand that this is what he is supposed to do. Always take him on leash so you will be there to see what he did and reward a successful potty event.

Step 5 – When he makes a mistake, clean it up and don't punish your puppy. Just totally ignore that he did it, and make a mental decision to do a better job of managing him next time.

Step 6 – Keep records of what happens each day. Note times and places of any accidents, and the reason it happened so that you can spot a pattern that you can fix. This will also help you see how well your puppy is doing.

APPENDIX A: TROUBLESHOOTING

MY PUPPY IS PEEING AND/OR POOPING IN HIS CRATE.

Make sure your crate is not too large. Your puppy must not have enough room to soil in the corner and still have a clean place to sleep. The crate should be large enough to turn around and lie down in, but no more. If your crate is the correct size, then check whether you are leaving him in the crate too long. Some dogs simply can't hold it very long during the beginning of training. If you are sure you are getting him out regularly enough (this might mean every half hour for a bit), then you should take your puppy to the vet to rule out any health issues. If the vet gives the puppy a clean bill of health, then you probably should contact a professional dog trainer for help. One of the best ways to locate a good trainer is to go to www.APDT.com (the website of the Association of Professional Dog Trainers), and do a "Trainer Search".

MY PUPPY WAKES ME UP MANY TIMES A NIGHT.

If your puppy is older than twelve weeks, he may be feeling like a bit of nighttime fun is good. Be sure to restrict his water after 7 in the evening, and to play with him during the evening to get him tired. Take him out for his last walk as late as you can. If he gets you up and doesn't go potty when you take him out, be sure you aren't fun at all. Don't talk to him (except if he does go potty), don't look at him, just take him out and then put him away after giving him time to go. If he cries again, ignore him, unless it's at a time when he has shown he normally goes when you take him out. You may need to ignore him for a number of times, but he will give it up as long as you don't pay any attention to him (that includes trying to soothe him or yelling at him).

I CAN'T BE HOME TO DO THE SCHEDULE LIKE YOU DESCRIBE.

I'm afraid that it will be impossible to train a puppy if you can't have someone there several times during the day, especially for a young puppy or small dog. Try hiring a dog walker for a couple of months until your dog is able to hold it for longer. Remember that dogs need more than just to go to the bathroom during the day. They need exercise and company also, especially if they are young. An alternative to a dog walker/sitter is doggy daycare, if your puppy is old enough and has had all of its shots. This can be a great solution for working people – the puppy comes home tired and won't be a crazy maniac from boredom all day.

Another solution would be to paper/pad/litter train your dog. I don't recommend this to anyone who ultimately doesn't want the dog to go inside, since it is so hard to train a dog to stop doing something they have been doing routinely for a while. Sometimes this is a good permanent solution for smaller dogs, though. If you decide to do this, follow the directions on the product you are using. Training for litter boxes and pads is beyond the scope of this booklet.

MY DOG WAS HOUSETRAINED BUT NOW HE IS HAVING ACCIDENTS.

The very first thing to do when this happens is to have your vet check for any health related issues, such as a urinary tract infection. If your vet has given your dog a clean bill of health, then take a look at your dog's life lately. Has anything changed? Have you moved, is there a new person or animal in the house? Has there been any change in your schedule? Many times, when there has been a disruption in a dog's life, he will begin having accidents in the house. This is not due to spite, but rather to stress. If you can't figure out what's going on, or how to fix it, you should contact a professional dog trainer for help. One of the best ways to locate a good trainer is to go to www.APDT.com (the website of the Association of Professional Dog Trainers), and do a "Trainer Search". Also keep in mind that as a dog reaches old age, he often becomes incontinent. Again, check with your vet to be sure there is nothing else going on. For an old dog, it's often best to confine him to a small room with toys and a comfy bed when you can't be with him, such as a bathroom, where it's easy to clean up. There may not be anything else to be done at that point.

I TAKE MY PUPPY FOR LONG WALKS AND THEN HE COMES IN AND GOES IN THE HOUSE.

First, you shouldn't be taking your puppy for a walk until AFTER he eliminates. No fun until he's empty! Secondly, you may be teaching your puppy that the fun is over after he goes by rushing him into the house and in his crate after he goes potty. Make a point of playing a bit or going for a short walk when he's done, and he won't see going potty as the end of being outside, where there is so much to do and smell and see. If you do this, you'll find that he begins to go right away so that he can have the play or walk sooner.

I TAKE MY PUPPY TO THE POTTY SPOT BUT HE DOESN'T GO.

When you take him to his area, stand quietly in one spot and let him sniff around there, but not pull you somewhere else. Be extremely boring – don't talk to him or look at him until he begins to eliminate. If you are out for five minutes and your puppy hasn't eliminated, take him in and crate him for 15 minutes, and then try again. Do not let him out or have any fun until he has done his business. When he does, have a party! Treats, praise, running around, whoo-pee!!! Make going potty a blast! Not going is dull, going starts the fun! Keep in mind that if you have punished him for going in front of you inside, he may have become afraid to go when you are around. This is one of the big reasons to ignore mistakes – the puppy will often get the wrong message (he figures it's not eliminating in the house that's the problem, it's eliminating in the house *while you are there* that gets him punished).

MY PUPPY ALWAYS SNEAKS OFF TO GO WHERE I CAN'T SEE HIM IN THE HOUSE.

First, you must not be watching him like a hawk if he can sneak out of sight. Make sure he doesn't get the opportunity. Second, you may have accidentally taught him that it isn't safe to pee in front of you by yelling or punishing him. This can result in him feeling that it's okay to go in the house as long as you aren't around, but not when you are. Not the lesson you want him to learn!

APPENDIX B: 10 COMMON HOUSETRAINING MISTAKES

1 – PUNISHING MISTAKES.

This creates confusion for your puppy, since he does not understand what you are trying tell him. You can also teach your dog that it is not safe to eliminate in front of you or bad things will happen, resulting in "sneak eliminations" when you aren't around, or in refusing to go when you are nearby, even outside. Don't punish your puppy, just clean it up and do better next time.

2 – NOT TAKING THE PUPPY OUT ON A LEASH.

If you aren't right there with him, you won't be able to re-ward him for success in time for him to connect the treat with the behavior. Also, you won't be able to create a "potty spot", which helps him to understand that you are out to eliminate, not just to sniff and play. Thirdly, if you aren't with him, you may not know if he has eliminated, which is necessary before he can have his supervised time outside of the crate.

3 – NOT REWARDING GOOD BEHAVIOR.

A critical key to success is teaching the puppy that it is VERY GREAT to eliminate outside. By giving a great treat and plenty of praise and attention, your puppy will want to do his business in his potty spot much sooner. Clients sometimes ask me if they should take treats with them every time the dog is outside, and I always ask, "Do you want your puppy to go potty outside more often? Then yes!" Praise is great, but for most puppies, treats are even better.

4 – NOT CLEANING UP ACCIDENTS PROPERLY.

Be sure to thoroughly clean up any mistakes your puppy makes in the house. Buy an enzymatic cleaner and follow the instructions so the smell of the spot won't attract your puppy to go there again. Do not use an ammonia-based cleaner.

5 – NOT PICKING A "POTTY SPOT".

Go to the same spot each time to help your puppy understand that here is where he is to do his business. This will help him learn to potty more quickly so that he can play or go for a walk.

6 – TAKING THE PUPPY INSIDE AND CRATING HIM AS SOON AS HE POTTIES.

Take a minute to play or walk with your puppy after he goes in his spot. If you rush him right into his crate, or even back in the house, he may begin to feel that the fun is over when he eliminates, and he will begin to take longer and longer to go. Teach him that fun *starts* when he is done pottying so that he will hurry up.

7 – KEEPING THE PUPPY IN TOO LARGE AN AREA WHEN NOT SUPERVISED.

Most people feel sorry for a puppy in a crate, but as long as you give him plenty of supervised playtime, he is fine in a small area and will most likely nap. His unsupervised area should be only large enough to turn around and lie down in, or else he can eliminate in the corner and still keep his sleeping area clean. Use his natural desire to stay clean to help you in your housetraining efforts.

8 – NOT WATCHING THE PUPPY CLOSELY ENOUGH DURING HIS PLAYTIME.

Your puppy should be the only thing you are watching while he is out of his crate. Your goal should be to have no accidents at all in the house, which means you must be alert to the first signs that he has to go so you can whisk him out to his potty area.

9 – NOT TAKING THE PUPPY OUT FREQUENTLY ENOUGH.

Sometimes people want their puppy to learn to "hold it" by not taking him out as often as necessary. He is holding it in the crate in order to keep his sleeping area clean, but while he is having his supervised playtime, he must go out for potty breaks constantly. An active puppy may have to go every 10-15 minutes, so get him outside frequently to avoid accidents. As he gets a bit older, you can spread the breaks out for longer times, but at first, there is no such thing as too many times out to potty.

10 – THINKING THE JOB IS DONE TOO SOON.

Many times people think that because their puppy hasn't had an accident for a while, that he is fully housetrained. This is often not the case. If you have been managing the puppy's life properly by crating him and supervising him with lots of potty breaks, he has been learning that going outside is best, but he may not actually be fully trained yet. You may find that if no one takes him out when he needs to go, he will just go in the house anyway. The trick is to continue to supervise his time out of the crate but to extend the time between his potty trips a little at a time. Also, be very careful to notice if he is beginning to signal when he needs to go out. If he learns that you will notice his signals, he will begin to trust that you will let him out. In general, you shouldn't consider your dog fully housetrained until you haven't had a single accident in the house for at least two months.

APPENDIX C: YOUR DOG'S FOOD

Feeding your puppy a good quality puppy food will actually help your housetraining. Cheap dog food has lots of fillers, which causes your dog to have more waste and he will need to eliminate more. Good quality food gives your dog nice firm stools, shiny hair, bright eyes, and overall vitality.

Unfortunately, most foods sold in grocery stores and the big pet food chains are low quality, even the ones that claim to be "premium". In fact, some of the brands vets recommend are not very high quality for the price. Be sure to check the ingredients before deciding what to feed your puppy. The first ingredient should be a protein such as beef, lamb, chicken, turkey. Meal is okay, but not by-products (these may include things like beaks and feathers, ick). There should be minimal grains, and you should not buy food with corn, wheat, soy, and white rice – these are unhealthy fillers for dogs. Avoid sweeteners like beet pulp, and artificial colors and preservatives. The food should be preserved with tocopherols, Vitamin E. Your dog will benefit from a high quality food, and this will save you money on vet bills over his lifetime.

AFTERWORD

FREE BONUS! Be sure to go to www.ReallySimpleDogTraining.com/HSFBonus.html to get your FREE printable record keeping sheet. You'll also get a surprise free bonus to help you in your housetraining efforts!

I wish you the best in your efforts to housetrain your puppy. If you diligently follow the steps outlined above, you should see positive results quickly. Just remember that you are teaching your puppy a new way to live, and that this takes time. Patience and a sense of humor are your best tools!

If you enjoyed this booklet, I invite you to write a short review on Amazon to help others find success in their housetraining endeavors. Also I recommend checking out my two training books, "Dog Training Made Simple: A Professional Dog Trainer Shares Her Secrets" and "Puppy Training: 6 Weeks to a Better-Behaved Puppy" for Amazon Kindle. They are laid out in different formats, covering some of the same material, but not all. "Dog Training" is broken into sections by behaviors you want to teach your dog, covering the steps to take the behavior from early stages to fully trained, while "Puppy Training" covers those behaviors and more in a weekly progressive training program, with additional information on important topics for puppy owners.

If you feel you are ready for more intensive training with your puppy, be sure to take a look at "COME HERE! Teach Your Dog To Come When You Call". This is advanced training in recalling, leash walking, "Leave It" work, and teaches an "Emergency Down". These are skills that can save your dog's life!

Be sure to look for more booklets in the series *"Really Simple Dog Training"*, coming soon!

Carol Miller, CDT

www.ReallySimpleDogTraining.com

CLAIM YOUR FREE BONUS

FREE BONUS!

Be sure to go to

www.ReallySimpleDogTraining.com/HSFBonus.html

to get your FREE printable record keeping sheet. You'll also get a surprise free bonus to help you in your housetraining efforts!

Puppy Training

Six Weeks to a Better-Behaved Puppy

A "Really Simple Dog Training" Booklet

By: Carol Miller, CDT

BEFORE YOU START

Welcome to the fun world of training your puppy! This program is based on my beginning "Basics" training course, and will help you get your puppy on his way to becoming a great family pet. Before we get started, there are a few things you need to know, so be sure to take the time to read the introductory sections before jumping right in. I'll keep it short, because I know you're excited and eager to get started!

Expectations

First, I want to be quite clear - you cannot take a puppy and turn him into a perfect dog in six weeks. But you can greatly improve his behavior while setting him up to become better and better. If you follow these instructions, you will know how to keep working with him to get him more and more reliable. Just keep in mind that puppies are young, and are easily distracted, and will not be able to focus like an adult dog (think 5 year olds - no matter how hard you try, you can't turn one into a mature adult because they are simply too young).

When your puppy goes through adolescence (around 7 months to 2-3 years old), you will likely see an increase in bad behaviors you thought you had fixed, and possibly some new ones. This is normal (think TEENAGER!), but if you have done your homework with him and hold firm to your boundaries, you will have a much easier time of it. Teenaged dogs are the ones most likely to be put in shelters, since many owners make the mistake of letting small puppies get away with things like jumping on them and pulling on the leash, but when they quickly become larger, these behaviors seem unmanageable.

Do yourself a favor: imagine your small puppy as a big dog, even if it's a yorkie. When he does something, ask yourself if it would be acceptable if he were 90 pounds, and if not, don't let him do it even if he's tiny. It's so much easier to change something that hasn't become an entrenched habit!

Training Basics

In this program, we are using positive reinforcement training, which is based in science. These are the most important points to remember:

- Reward behavior you want to see more of
- Avoid your puppy practicing behavior you don't like
- Replace bad behavior with something you would rather your puppy do
- Set your puppy up for success - be sure he is able to do what you ask

Rewards

We will be using lots of treats, but will be working on phasing them out as the puppy gets proficient at something. For example, I rarely give my dogs a treat for sitting on command, but when I'm working on a new trick, then I use lots of treats. Treats are an easy way to let your puppy know he did something right, and most puppies respond eagerly to working for treats. You must pay attention to when he begins to show that he really understands what you've asked, and then start treating him for three sits in a row rather than only one, for example. Or even better, reward him for faster sits, and not for slow, sloppy ones.

With the exception of luring your dog into a position at the beginning of training something new, you should never show your puppy you have a treat. Waving a treat at your puppy to get him to do something will lead to him checking to see if you have a treat before deciding to obey. You want him to see you as a bit of a slot machine - maybe THIS time will be the one, which means you can't show treats ahead of time. Wear a treat bag, or better yet, have little containers of treats hidden out of his reach throughout the area the puppy is allowed in, so that you can just pop one out for him as a surprise.

We will also be using "real life rewards" to reward your puppy. Things like throwing his ball, going outside, and jumping into the car can all be used to reward your puppy. Rewards are something the puppy wants badly enough to work for.

Clicker/Marker Training Basics

In this program I will be using Marker Training, which is the same as Clicker Training except that you use a word like "Yes!" instead of a clicking sound. If you wish to use a clicker, just substitute "click" when you read "mark". I believe that a clicker is more effective than a verbal marker, but I've found that most of my clients have too much to manage without trying to handle a clicker as well.

First, you must understand that the "mark" doesn't mean "good dog". Rather, it tells your dog that what he did at that exact moment was what you were looking for, and will earn him a treat. The mark is always paired with a treat, and will be shortened to M/T, meaning "mark and treat your dog". At first your dog will not know that's what you mean, but he will figure it out quickly, and will begin to try to guess what he needs to do to get you to M/T.

You can see from this that your timing will be critical to your dog's understanding of what you want. If he does a sit for you when asked and you wait until he begins to get up again to M/T, he will probably think that "Sit" means "Sit and get up", or maybe just the get up part. You have confused him and slowed his learning down.

You can practice your timing by bouncing a tennis ball and saying your marker word as the ball hits the floor. Also, before you begin a training session, have a clear idea of what you are looking for, so you know what to mark.

To mark a behavior, at the exact moment he does what you are asking, say "Yes!" and give him a treat. The mark gives you time to hand the dog his treat (no later than 1 second or so, the sooner after the mark the better). After you have released him you can touch and praise him, but during the training you should do no more than say a soft "Good dog". You don't want to excite him into forgetting what he's doing.

Marking a behavior is only used in the beginning stages of learning, to help your dog figure out what you are look-ing for. Once he has figured it out, you no longer need to mark the behavior. However, if you are working on im-proving it, you should go back to marking it, since the behavior is now being learned under different circumstances. For example, once you have taught your dog to sit on command in the kitchen while you are standing in front of him, you don't need to mark the sit anymore. But if you decide to work on getting him to sit on your deck on command, you should go back to marking, since this is a new challenge for him.

Equipment

For this program, you will need a regular buckle or clip collar, a six foot leash, a treat bag (you can use a carpenter's nail apron from a hardware store - much cheaper than an "official" dog treat pouch), and a flat mat or dog bed (no puffy beds or beds with sides). You can use a carpet sample, a towel, a small floor mat - anything that's a bit bigger than your puppy and is easy for him to walk onto. Be sure you don't mind if it gets chewed on, which may happen at first.

If you have a strong puller, you should get a front-clip harness. These are much better than the harness where you hook the leash onto the dog's back, since those just let the dogs really put their shoulders into pulling you. With the leash attached to the front and passing around the shoulder, when the dog pulls, they are turned back toward you and away from what they are pulling to, and the harder they pull, the more they get turned away.

Some people find that the difference this makes is good enough that they don't need or want to do the work involved in teaching their dog not to pull. But it is important to remember that this is a management tool - it doesn't teach the dog not to pull, it just makes pulling not work so well when he's wearing it. You can find the Premier Easy-Walk harness at most pet stores, or order a

Sense-ation or Sense-ible harness online through http://www.softouchconcepts.com.

Management

Management is your first job with a puppy. For housetraining and to prevent inappropriate chewing, he should be in a small confined area unless he is being watched like a hawk. You can find advice on housetraining in my booklet "Housetraining Success Formula: 6 Simple Steps to Housetraining Your Puppy or Dog" available for Amazon Kindle.

Since most puppy problems result from too much freedom too soon, a crate or other small area is essential (See Appendix A for information on crate training). Just be sure that your puppy gets plenty of time to play, train and generally be a dog as well as being confined. He should be on a schedule where he is out with someone's full attention on him at regular intervals during the day.

When out of his crate or confinement area, he should only be in one room, so use baby gates and closed doors to be sure he can't run around the house and get into trouble where you can't see him. Pick things up so he doesn't learn the fun game of "Chase me, I've got your shoe!".

Make it very easy for him to be a good puppy and not to learn bad habits. Have plenty of good chew toys, and put some of them away so you can rotate which ones he has in order to keep him from getting bored with them. Toys that involve both of you, like tuggies and balls, should be put away unless you are using them. It's important that he think they are your toys that you share with him, not the other way around.

As he gets older and shows that he is no longer trying to chew on your furniture or steal things, you can begin to give him more freedom. But don't rush this. He needs to earn your trust.

Leadership

I only mention this because so many people have heard that you must "be the pack leader" in order to have a good dog. What you actually need to do is to "control the resources". Once your puppy understands that all good things in his life come from you, you will have his full attention. After all, it's true - he eats, drinks, goes out, has toys, has company, gets bones, and plays games all because you provide this for him.

Think of is as being a parent. When your kids are babies and small children, they do what you say, provided you are firm about it. But when they get older, they begin to challenge you. If you have set up rules that have consequences like "no cell phone privileges" or "no trips to the mall" if the rules are broken, your teenager takes this into consideration and is more likely to stay in line. They know you control their life, and even though they may want to do something you've forbidden, they don't want the consequences of disobedience, and (most of the time) will do what you ask.

Your puppy is the same. When he is tiny, he happily comes when you call him, but when he is older he starts to make a decision - "Hmm," he thinks, "This is a great smell. I like you, but I see you all the time, so - Later, Dude". If you've taught him that all good things in his life come from you, you'll see much less of this.

51

In this program, we don't use punishment or intimidation, but we do set boundaries and requirements for behavior. By using rewards to encourage what we want to see, we build good habits in our puppy, and when needed, we are firm about what we want. If your puppy gets too worked up and is biting your hands, put him in his crate or area calmly and without anger, and let him settle down before he comes out. If he is barking or crying, do not let him out, or he is training you to open the door when he barks or whines. Be firm and patient, but not angry or loud. Just outwait him.

Socialization

I can't say enough about the importance of socialization. This is the process of getting your puppy exposed to new things. Although this is especially important early on, it should be a life-long process in order to avoid him developing fears. Socialization involves having your puppy meet lots of people, other puppies and friendly dogs, going to new places, walking on all types of surfaces (shiny floors, gravel, sidewalks, soft surfaces, wobbly surfaces, etc.), walking near bicyclers, skateboarders, motorcyclists, walking in towns and the woods, visiting the vet's office just to say "hi", rides in the car, etc.

You can purchase CD's with scary noises like fireworks, barking dogs, thunder, baby cries and motorcycles and play them at low levels to help your puppy get used to them.

Your vet might have warned you to keep your puppy indoors until he has all of his shots, but many experts say that more dogs are killed by lack of socialization than ever die of diseases. This is due to the difficult problem behaviors that can result from fear, such as aggression, which all too often ends up with the dog euthanized. You can expose your dog to the world without taking chances on disease if you do it carefully. Of course, if your puppy is older, you don't have to worry as much. Here are some ways to safely socialize your puppy:

- Have a party, have music and decorations, and pass your puppy around among your friends
- Go to the entrance of a busy store and let strangers handle your cute puppy
- Take your puppy to kids' indoor meetings and let the kids pet your puppy
- Take your puppy for drives in the car (seat belted or crated safely)
- Tether him in a wagon or a stroller (or carry him if he's small) and take walks in the country or a park
- Once he has enough shots, join a puppy socialization class
- When he's completed this course, take him to a group class in a pet store or training facility to practice his skills in a noisy, distracting environment with other dogs and people

Stages of learning: Kinda got it (beginning), Got it when nothing much else is happening (intermediate), Got it no matter what (expert).

One of the biggest mistakes people make when training their dog is to assume the job is done too soon. When you have just taught your dog something (for example "Sit"), very quickly he will be responding nicely to your command. What you must keep in mind is that he is really making his best guess as to what will get him a reward.

If you keep practicing and rewarding, he will soon pass from the "kinda got it" stage into the "got it as long as nothing else interesting is going on" stage. At this point, he can reliably sit when asked, provided there are no other people in the room, he's not outside where he has a world of smells, sights and sounds to pay attention to, there's nothing interesting on the floor, etc. etc. etc. You might say that he will easily do it for you as long as there is nothing strong pulling him away from you. Important: the stronger you train this foundation, the easier it will be for your dog to handle distractions as you train them.

Distractions are anything that might be going on in the environment that could cause your puppy to forget what he's doing. The ability to obey even around the most intense distractions (other dogs, squirrels, deer, moving toys, running children, etc.) is what makes the difference between a dog who is somewhat trained versus a dog who has been trained completely.

To move into the next stage takes more work. You must systematically teach him that he not only can but wants to pay attention when other things are in his environment. Doing this successfully involves stepping through the levels of difficulty as opposed to jumping up to hard levels without the steps in between.

Let's go back to our "Sit" example. Your puppy can easily sit when asked in the living room when you are alone and no toys are out. You now add a small distraction, and reward him nicely for being able to sit during this. A small distraction might be your spouse in the room sitting quietly in a chair not looking at the dog. When he performs a sit on command like this 8 times out of 10, you can make it a bit harder. Your spouse might stand up near where your puppy is. They might make a small movement. They might make a quiet noise. As your puppy succeeds 8 times out of 10 for each of these things, you can make it slightly harder. In a relatively short period of time you can move through quite a few levels, but if you had skipped the steps, your puppy might not be able to perform correctly.

You want to go slowly enough that he says to himself, "Oh, it's just like the last time I did it, only slightly harder. I can do that!" Eventually you can reach a point where your puppy will respond any time, any place – provided that you have trained him to do so. Don't worry too much about this – this process is built into the progression of exercises in this book.

Tips for Better Training

Make it fun. Have a good time with it. Use a happy voice and think of training as playing games with your puppy. The more both of you see training as a game, the better your training will go. If you don't feel like it, don't do it - your puppy will feel that it's not fun for you and it won't be fun for him either. If he can't focus, ask for something really easy so he can end on a good note, and stop for now.

Keep it short. Training should be in small sessions. Your puppy has a baby attention span, and can't focus for long periods of time. Three five minute sessions are more effective than one fifteen minute one. Again, if you see your puppy losing focus, ask for something that's easy for him and stop.

Keep it simple. Always begin something new in a quiet area with no distractions. That means pick up his toys and chewies, turn off the TV, put any other pets away, and make sure there's nothing else for him to focus on. As he gets better at a behavior, you will be adding distractions to your work with him, but always start off so it's easy for him to concentrate.

Mix training into your puppy's everyday life. You don't want your puppy to think that he only listens to you during "training time", so be sure to ask him for things as part of his normal routine. Want me to pet you? Sure, just sit first. Throw that ball? Lie down, please. Right from the start you'll be introducing the "Nothing in Life Is Free" policy - this is how you get a dog who loves to do things for you, since he's always getting great things when he does! You should keep doing this exercise for the rest of his life, as it is one of the best ways to maintain good boundaries for your dog.

Remember that just because you taught him the beginning steps of something doesn't mean he can do it in any circumstances. Always keep the "kinda got it", "got it when nothing much else is happening" and " got it no matter what" stages in mind. Your puppy will still be in the "kinda got it/got it when nothing much else is happening" stages for quite a while. It takes practice and commitment on your part to get to the "really got it" stage. Don't expect that if you haven't trained it.

Set your puppy up for success. This goes hand-in-hand with the previous tip. Don't ask for things your puppy can't do. If he's outside in the yard smelling something really great, don't call him. Do something noisy that will make him curious to come to see what you are doing, or go get him. Don't teach him to ignore you by asking him for things you haven't taught yet. As you teach him to do something harder, you want to move in tiny steps. Each time he should think, "Oh, that's just like what I've already done, just a bit different". By taking tiny steps you can move quickly, since nothing is totally new and too much more difficult for him. If you're having difficulty getting/keeping his attention, wait until he is hungrier to train, using better treats. Remember the treats are needed only until you have built his strong habit of listening and working with you.

Remember, he's just learning. Even if it's trying to get him to stop jumping on you, he's just learning. If he's still doing it, he hasn't learned it yet under those conditions. It's information for you - "Note to self: need to work on this some more". Don't lose your cool; just make a plan to address the problem. You wouldn't scold and yell at a child for having trouble with his homework (at least I hope not) - you would try to help, maybe get him a tutor. It's the same for your puppy - he is struggling with learning how to do things a different way.

See things from his point of view. Puppies are born wanting constant attention, needing to chew on everything. They think any absorbent surface is a great potty spot, and generally are just natural beings - baby dogs. To live successfully in our human world, they need to learn our rules, which are usually totally contrary to their natural drives. "I'm excited to see you, I should jump all over you!", "I have to go potty, here's a great spot on the rug!", "Man that chair looks like it would feel good if I chewed it!", "That hand looks like fun, I think I'll try to grab it!" - these are things your puppy naturally thinks. Since we have to teach him to do things differently, try to be fair to him and not expect him to do it without you helping. Use management to prevent most problems, and teach him what you want for everything else.

Don't be in a hurry. Take the time to build strong foundations, and when you get to harder training, it will be much easier. This program is set up as a six week long training plan, but you are not obligated to do it in that timeframe. Your own schedule, your puppy's ability to concentrate, and many other things may make it better to take longer on each week's lesson. Let your dog tell you when it's time to move on by how well he's doing.

WEEK ONE

Things to accomplish this week:

- Understand the principles of positive reinforcement training
- Focus on setting the puppy up for success
- Learn to see what the puppy is doing that you LIKE rather than what you don't like
- Determine the best reinforcers for your puppy – figure out what HE likes best. Pay attention to how he reinforces himself during the day
- Begin to create a clear system of communication with your puppy to avoid confusing him
- Teach your puppy to respond to his name
- Teach "Sit"
- Play the "Collar Grab" game
- Begin to train him to come when called
- Begin to work on impulse control - "Leave It", Stage One
- Require the "Nothing In Life Is Free" policy – Sit for everything
- Socialization checklist

Positive Reinforcement Training

Positive reinforcement training, also called positive training, not only teaches your puppy to do specific tasks, but also builds your relationship with him. Positive training is fun for both you and your puppy, and fosters cooperation and a desire to work together. Old-fashioned techniques such as leash-jerking, spraying with water guns, choke and prong collars, scolding and hitting may cut back on behaviors you don't like in the short run, but in the long run they cause your puppy to be afraid of you, and many times actually create new problems in your puppy, such as aggression. If you train with kindness and respect, and your puppy will learn to love working with you.

We use lots of reinforcement when training a puppy. When we talk about reinforcement, we mean things that reward your puppy for a behavior. When you give your puppy a treat for sitting nicely, you are reinforcing that behavior, which means it becomes more likely to happen again.

There are many types of reinforcement in your puppy's life. You provide some - treats, games, attention, etc. - but much of the reinforcement from his life is coming from outside of you. When your puppy barks at people walking past your house, he is getting reinforced by the rush he feels, and possibly by the feeling of chasing them away. When your puppy sniffs a tree during a walk, he is taking his reinforcement from his environment.

To help your training process, it is important to try to have as much reinforcement come through you as possible. Through management, you can control how your puppy reinforces himself. The very first step is to notice just how much your puppy gets his rewards from outside of you.

Since the basic principle of how animals learn, is "REINFORCEMENT BUILDS BEHAVIOR", we want to do the following:

- Reward the puppy for behaviors you want to see more of
- Avoid the puppy practicing things you don't want him to do (management)
- Take control of his environmental reinforcers
- Set your puppy up for success – don't make an exercise too hard for him

Learn to understand what your puppy is telling you – you may not be correct about what he really likes, so pay attention to his reactions to various things such as treats and petting.

Be very clear and consistent so that your puppy can understand what you want – don't use more than one command for the same thing, such as "come" one time and "come here" the next.

THINGS TO DO THIS WEEK

First Day: Pay attention to what your puppy does right.
Today, put 25 small treats in your pocket. Watch your puppy as he goes about his day. Whenever you see him doing something you think is good behavior, say "Yes!" and give him a treat. This includes chewing on his own toys, sitting quietly at your feet, coming up to you without jumping up, going potty outside – anything that you think is good behavior.

First Couple of Days: Figure out what your puppy likes best.
Find out what your puppy really likes – these are the things that you will use to motivate him to do things you ask. While there are many different kinds of treats sold in the stores, your puppy may not particularly like them, especially since most are made from grains and corn. Puppies most often prefer smelly treats, such as meat or cheese.

Store-bought treats are almost always too big. You should be using small pieces, pea-sized or smaller, for training treats. Take several different types of treats, such as bits of meat, cheese, cheerios, commercial treats, pizza crusts, croutons, etc. Put a different one in each hand and offer both to your puppy. Try to determine which he likes best by which he picks. Create a list of what he likes the best. Of course, some puppies like everything, which is just fine.

Also, pay attention to your puppy's body language when you pet him. Does he lean into it and ask for more when you stop, or does he stiffen and pull away? If he pulls away, he isn't comfortable with what you're doing, so try to pet him differently. Most puppies dislike being petted on the top of the head (although scratching and rubbing is more likely to be fine). Try rubbing his chest, or the sides of his face. Move slowly and calmly. Remember, if he doesn't like what you're doing, it's not a reward!

First Couple of Days: Understand your puppy's environmental reinforcers.

Watch your puppy and see how many times a day he takes reinforcement from the environment. See what he finds fun and interesting, and pay extra attention to those that have nothing to do with you. Barking out the window, sniffing a tree, running free in the backyard, chasing the cat – all of these things are reinforcing to your puppy, and you need to be aware of them.

Each Day: Play the "Name Game".

Several times a day, when you see your puppy mildly distracted, say his name and give him a treat for looking at you. You are teaching him to pay attention to you, which is the foundation for everything that comes later. Build his habit of looking at you when you say his name. Remember not to use his name much when you are not expecting him to look at you.

Each Day: "Sit" Exercise.

Begin by getting prepared – be in a quiet room with no distractions, and have tasty treats in your pocket or treat pouch. Put a treat in your hand. Get your puppy's attention and start with him standing in front of you. Take the treat and hold it just at his nose, and with him following it, move the treat slightly up and toward his back, easing him into a sit.

Do not say anything as you do this! If you say "Sit", or worse, "Sit, sit, sit", you will just teach him to ignore that sound. Since at this stage, he doesn't even know what you want him to do, keep quiet and simply lure him into a sit.

At the instant his bottom hits the floor, say "Yes!" and give him the treat. Then say "Free" and move a bit to show him he can get up. "Sit" should mean "Sit there until I tell you to do something different", so remember to give it a beginning and an end. Do this a few times until he shows he is starting to understand by easily sitting as you move the treat.

Now it's time to stop using a treat to lure him. Hide a treat in your other hand, and pretend to lure him as you have been doing. Since your hand will still smell like treats and he is expecting to sit down, he will most likely sit the same way he has been while being lured. Say "Yes!" and quickly give him the treat from the other hand, then release him with "Free". Repeat this several times until he shows that he is "getting it" by sitting when you move your hand as if luring (no food in it, remember) 8 times out of 10.

If he stops sitting with your hand signal, use the food lure again once or twice, then go back to using your hand without food. Always have a treat in your other hand so you can quickly reward the correct behavior with a M/T (mark/treat, "Yes!" followed by the treat from your other hand).

As he begins to get better at this, begin to wait a bit longer before marking and treating, first one second, then two, etc. If he gets up before you mark or release him, you are extending the time too fast, so shorten the time for a while and then try again.

Have several short sessions each day, using the hand signal to ask for the sit. After he is doing well with a hand signal, begin to teach the verbal command. Say the word "Sit" a half second BEFORE using the hand signal. Be sure to reward your puppy each time, saying "Yes!" immediately as his bottom touches the floor, then give him a treat. Quickly say "Free" and move to release him from the sit.

Do this in a place that is quiet and has no distractions to help set him up for success. Remember, if you can't reward him for doing it right, he isn't learning anything.

Each Day: Play the "Collar Grab" game.
Sit your puppy in front of you, and have a treat hidden in one hand. Reach for his collar (at the side of his body, not over his head) with your free hand. Take it gently, and while holding it, give him the treat with your other hand. Let go. Repeat 4 or 5 times in a session. If your puppy is hand shy or nervous about this, start by just moving your hand by the side of his face, then give the treat. Gradually work up to reaching to just touch the collar, then gently holding it.

You should use a collar grab every time you do a recall with your puppy. It is important to be able to grab your puppy when you need to, and this game also helps nervous puppies get used to hands coming at them.

Each Day: Play "Recall" games with your puppy.
The best way to work on getting your puppy to love coming to you is to play recall games. By having your puppy

come to you for fun and treats, he will begin to love running to you, and you will be most of the way there.

Chase Me Game – This is a game one person can play with a puppy anytime they are in a safe, enclosed area such as in the house or in a fenced yard. Have some tasty treats in one hand. Get your puppy's attention and toss a treat behind you (to give you a head start), saying "Get It!", and as he eats the treat, run quickly in the opposite direction, calling him in a fun, happy voice. Be silly, slap your legs, make funny noises – anything that your puppy thinks is fun and will help him run after you. When he reaches you, stop and praise and give him a treat.

Always be sure to give him the treat very close to you, and grab his collar at the same time to get him used to the fact that you might grab him after calling. It does no good to teach your puppy to come and stay just out of reach, so insist that he comes all the way so that you can grab him, and then let go, toss another treat behind you and play again. Play this a few times in a row, but don't play so much that your puppy gets bored. Always leave him wanting to play more.

Back and Forth Game – This is the two or more person version of the "Chase Me" Game. Start with two people around 6 feet apart in a quiet enclosed area. Each person should have some tasty treats hidden in their hand. The first person should call the puppy in a happy, fun voice, and run away a little to encourage the puppy to chase him. When he arrives, treat him close in with a grab of his collar, and while he's eating, the next person should call him the same way. Soon your puppy will be happily running back and forth for fun and treats.

You can add other people to this game now, calling the puppy to each of you in random order. Be sure this is fun and happy and you stop before your puppy gets bored.

Your goal is to make coming when called fun and extremely rewarding for your puppy.

Remember that he always has to decide whether coming to you is better than whatever else he is doing, so you want to quickly establish that you are the best choice. Remember to ALWAYS notice when he comes to you, and NEVER punish or scold him, even if he brings you a chewed up slipper. If you scold him when he arrives, he will begin to think coming to you isn't a good thing at all, so don't do it!!!

Be sure to use a happy voice and the same word each time you call him. And don't call him if you don't think he'll come.

Each Day: Work on Impulse Control with the "Leave It" game.

Leave It Game Stage One: With several low value treats in one hand (such as kibbles) and your puppy sitting in front of you, say "Leave It" and then offer your treat hand to your puppy. As he grabs for the treats, close your hand quickly, being sure he does not get a treat. Let him sniff, lick, paw, nibble and even bite at your hand – don't move at all, don't say anything.

Wait until he stops trying to get at the food out of frustration, then quickly open your hand and give him another chance at it. Go through the process again until he gives up, and then open your hand again. When he finally figures out that trying to take a treat won't get him one and he doesn't move at it, pick a treat up with your other hand

and feed it to him. If he tries for the treats again, repeat the process.

Keep this up until you can feed him the treats one at a time without him trying to get them himself. Be sure to only say the command once, at the beginning of the exercise.

CRITICAL TIP: PUPPY NEVER GETS TO WIN BY GRABBING.

Each Day: Do "Nothing In Life Is Free" with your puppy.

Every single time your puppy wants something, wait for a sit. Don't ask for it, just wait until he does it and then say, "Yes!" and give him what it is that he is sitting for. Situations you should use this for include:
- Putting his food bowl down
- Getting out of his crate or confined area
- Going outside
- Getting his leash on or off
- Getting a new chew bone
- Playing with a toy
- Snuggling with you
- Before he gets in or out of the car
- Before he can greet guests

This one exercise helps to build your puppy's self-control and helps him see that he is not the one who makes the rules. All members of the family should do this simple thing. Very shortly your puppy will figure out that sitting gets him what he wants, and he will begin to sit quickly anytime he wishes you to do something for him. Soon he will figure that if he doesn't know what you want from him, sit might be a good idea. This is great for you, since when your puppy is sitting, he's not jumping on you, begging, biting at your ankles, etc. This is one of the most important things you can teach your puppy, so be sure to do it.

Socialization Checklist:

- Did you take him somewhere new this week?
- Did he meet at least two new people this week?
- Did he see at least two new things this week (like umbrellas, people wearing hats, roller skaters)?
- Did he walk on lots of different surfaces this week?
- Did he play with other puppies or friendly dogs this week?

Remember: Keep sessions short and fun!

WEEK TWO

Things to accomplish this week:

- Think about how clearly you are communicating with your puppy, and work on becoming clearer
- Teach your puppy to recognize both visual and verbal commands
- Increase the level of difficulty of "Sit"
- Improve your puppy's response to his name
- Teach "Down"
- Improve the recall
- Practice impulse control - "Leave It", Stage Two
- Begin teaching leash manners
- Work on greeting manners – start to teach your puppy not to jump on people
- Begin to train the "Silent Stay"
- Continue to require the "Nothing In Life Is Free" policy – Sit for everything
- Socialization checklist

Communication

It's very important to understand how your puppy perceives what you ask of him. It's tempting to call the puppy stupid or stubborn when he doesn't sit when you ask him, but most of the time, he simply doesn't know what you want from him. Confusion can come from one or more of several things:

- The puppy hasn't fully learned the command
- You have asked for a behavior he knows, but something is different, and he doesn't understand
- You are not using consistent commands for the behavior
- You are saying a command but your body language is contradicting it

Many times puppy owners underestimate the time and repetitions it takes for a puppy to "know" a command. Although the puppy may do it correctly often, he is still guessing for quite some time. It takes hundreds, even thousands of repetitions for him to know a command absolutely, and even then it must be what we call "generalized", or taught in many places and under many conditions before he will be sure of what you want.

Also, if you ask the puppy to come to you but lean towards him, his natural instinct is to move away. Use these instincts to help the puppy do what you want – when you call him, move back away from him to draw him near.

Don't a use stern, gruff voice that may scare the puppy. Use high energy sounds for moving commands such as "Come", and soft, low, long ones for stationary commands like "Stay".

And of course, always use the same word for a command, never "Down" one time and "Lie Down" another, or worse, "Down" to lie down and also to get off of the couch or stop jumping on you.

THINGS TO DO THIS WEEK

Each Day: Pay attention to how you communicate with your puppy.
Notice your body language and work on being quieter, so you are not communicating anything unintentional with your puppy. Be sure to use the same commands each time you ask for a behavior. Check that everyone in the family knows what the commands are, so that everyone asking the puppy to do something is using the same word. Experiment a little with your body language – notice that if you move towards your puppy, he will tend to back away, and away from him he will likely follow. Begin to see how you can use this to help him do what you want, and to avoid sending mixed messages to him.

Each Day: Ask for a "Sit" with a verbal command only.
Start by saying "Sit" half of a second before using your hand signal. After ten or so repetitions, try saying "Sit" and DON'T use the hand signal. Give your puppy a few seconds to think about it, if needed. If he sits, praise and treat! If not, wait a few more seconds, then do the "Sit" and hand signal ten more times. Then try again without the hand signal.

Throughout the week, practice "Sit" with just the verbal command as well as with the hand signal. If he doesn't sit for the verbal command, wait and repeat the exercise as when you first added the verbal command described in this lesson. Then try again without the hand signal.

Practice "Sit" here and there throughout the day in different locations, but always when he is not very distracted. Remember to set your puppy up for success – make sure he is able to do what you ask. Be sure you are always using "Free" to release your puppy from the "Sit".

Each Day: Increase the difficulty of the "Name Game" a bit.

Like last week, several times a day, when you see your puppy mildly distracted, say his name and give him a treat for looking at you. Make a list of distractions for him (another person in the room, the TV on, toys on the floor, outside in the yard, a car driving past, etc.), and say his name during some of the milder distractions.

Don't do it for his hardest distractions yet – he won't be able to do it. For example, if seeing a squirrel is very distracting for him, don't try; however if he is outside with not much going on, try now.

Be sure to praise him as he turns his head, and treat him immediately when he looks at you. If you wait too long, he won't get the connection between what he did and the reward.

Each Day: Work on the "Down" Exercise.

To teach "Down", begin by getting prepared – be in a quiet room with no distractions, and have tasty treats in your pocket or treat pouch. Put a treat in your hand. Get your puppy's attention and start with him sitting in front of you. Take the treat and hold it just at his nose, and with him following it, move the treat down and in slightly toward his chest, easing him into a down, which means both ends of the puppy are on the ground, butt and elbows.

Do not say anything as you do this! If you say "Down", or worse, "Down, down, down", you will just teach him to

74

ignore that sound. Since at this stage, he doesn't even know what you want him to do, keep quiet and simply lure him into a down. At the instant his elbows hit the floor while his butt is still down, say "Yes!" and give him the treat. Then say "Free" and move a bit to show him he can get up.

"Down" should mean "Lie there until I tell you to do something different", so remember to give it a beginning and an end. Do this a few times until he shows he is starting to understand by easily lying down as you move the treat.

Now you must stop using a treat to lure him. Hide a treat in your other hand, and pretend to lure him as you have been doing. Since your hand will still smell like treats and he is expecting to lie down, he will most likely do a down the same way he has been while being lured. Say "Yes!" and quickly give him the treat from the other hand, then release him with "Free".

Repeat this several times until he shows that he is "getting it" by lying down when you move your hand as if luring (no food in it, remember) 8 times out of 10. If he stops lying down with your hand signal, use the food lure again once or twice, then go back to using your hand without food. Always have a treat in your other hand so you can quickly reward the correct behavior with an M/T (mark/treat, "Yes!" followed by the treat from your other hand).

Be sure to release the puppy quickly from the down by saying "Free" and moving. To help stretch the down out longer, quickly put treats between his feet before he can get up, and then release him. Gradually stretch out the time between treats. Have several short sessions each day, using the hand signal to lure him into the down.

Don't say "Down" yet. Be sure to reward your puppy each time, saying "Yes!" immediately as his body touches the floor (watch for elbows), then give him a treat. Do this in a place that is quiet and has no distractions to help set him up for success.

Once he can easily lie down with a hand signal, add the verbal command. Say the word "Down" a half second BEFORE using the hand signal. Do this 10 times in a row, then say "Down" and don't do the signal. Chances are good that your puppy will expect the signal and will just lie down - Hurray! Jackpot! If not, keep working on the "Down" followed by the hand signal a while longer, and then try again.

Remember, if you can't reward him for doing it right, he isn't learning anything. Don't forget to release him by saying "Free" and moving – both "Sit" and "Down" have a beginning and an end.

Each Day: Continue to play "Recall" games with your puppy.
Begin to call your puppy at random times during the day, when he's slightly distracted. Be sure to praise as he begins to come towards you, and treat when he arrives. Do this from different rooms of the house, and outside when he is less than five feet away from you and not distracted. Make a big deal out of it if he comes.

If he doesn't, DON'T call him again. Go to him and gently move him by the collar in the direction you were, and treat him for moving that way. Next time make it a bit easier and try again at that same distance after some more work.

Continue to play the "Chase Me Game" and the "Back and Forth Game" throughout the day. Remember to ALWAYS notice when he comes to you, and NEVER punish or scold him, even if he brings you a chewed up slipper. If you scold him when he arrives, he will begin to think coming to you isn't a good thing at all, so don't do it!!!

Be sure to use a happy voice and the same word each time you call him. And don't call if you don't think he'll come. A good recall takes tons of repetitions, and could save your puppy's life someday, so don't neglect this important exercise. Remember to grab your puppy's collar before giving him the treat - EVERY TIME.

Each Day: Practice Impulse Control.
Leave It Game Stage Two: Your puppy should be a champion at "Leave It" Stage One, treats in your hand. You are now going to increase the challenge for him. With your puppy sitting in front of you, say "Leave It" and place a small pile of low value treats on the floor in front of him. As he grabs for the treats, cover the pile with your hand quickly, being sure he does not get a treat. Let him sniff, lick, paw, nibble and even bite at your hand – don't move at all, don't say anything.

Wait until he stops trying to get at the food out of frustration, then quickly remove your hand and give him another chance at it. Go through the process again until he gives up, then remove your hand again. When he finally figures out that trying to take a treat won't get him one and he doesn't move at it, pick a treat up with your other hand and feed it to him. If he tries for the treats again, repeat the process.

Keep this up until you can feed him the treats one at a time without him trying to get them himself. Remember to only tell the puppy to "Leave It" at the beginning. Praise each time you feed him, and release him when you're done by saying "Free" and moving.

Each Day: Work on Beginning Leash Manners.
Exercise 1: Have high level treats in your hand. For just a few minutes several times a day, put your puppy on leash in your kitchen, bathroom, basement, or other place with very few distractions around. Don't go anywhere – just stand still and every time your puppy looks at you, say "Yes!" and give him a treat. Your goal is to begin to have your puppy feel that you matter when he is on leash – to most dogs the owner is simply a dead weight to be pulled around. With this exercise you are beginning to show the puppy that paying attention you to has value to him while he is leashed. If he won't stop staring at you, drop his treats on the floor so he has to look away and then back.

Exercise 2, first couple of days: Inside the house, with your puppy unleashed, put him in a sit. Pivot so that he is at your side, sitting facing the same direction as you are. Give him a treat every second or so for a short while to get him to feel great while at your side. The more he feels that's a great place to be, the easier it will be to teach him to walk nicely at your side. Repeat this exercise for just a minute or so a couple of times a day, if possible. If he gets up, don't worry about it, just start over. If you can't keep him there, you might need to use better treats for a bit until he begins to stay with you more.

Exercise 2, rest of the week: Inside the house, with your puppy unleashed, get your puppy in a sit at your side as described in Exercise 2 above. Treat your puppy a couple of times in this position. Then say "Free" and take one large step forward. If your puppy follows you, deliver a treat just as he arrives next to your leg. If he doesn't follow, pat your leg, make noises, etc. to encourage him to move toward you, and then treat when he arrives. Work toward moving around the house with your puppy moving into position with you. By the end of the week, you should have him walking nicely next to your side for at least 10 feet or so.

Start slowly, just a step at a time, and work up to several steps before treating. If your puppy wanders off, don't acknowledge it, just keep moving away from him, and he may join you again. If not, try again in a bit with better treats. If he continues to leave you, go back to the first stage of this exercise and build the value of sitting by your side more strongly. Remember never to say "No" or reprimand him for leaving you. This is an "error-less" exercise – we just build the good behavior up while ignoring any unwanted behaviors.

Each Day: Practice good greeting behavior.
If you can, try to get people to help you with greetings each day. Use all three methods to work on teaching your puppy not to jump on people. This should also be done with a family member the puppy jumps on when they come home.

Doorway method: Have the puppy confined elsewhere while you get set up. The guest should stand in a doorway inside the house, such as to a bathroom or bedroom. Release your puppy, and if the puppy jumps up, the guest quickly jumps back through the door and closes it, being careful not to hit the puppy. Wait a moment, then the guest should open the door and try again. If the puppy doesn't jump up, quickly give him a treat, a chance to say hi, and then take him away or give him a toy so he doesn't start jumping again. Repeat until the puppy can stay calm to receive a treat.

Tether method: Tether the puppy to a heavy piece of furniture or banister. As the guest moves towards him, if the puppy doesn't jump up, the guest continues toward him, gives a treat and a chance to say hi. If the puppy jumps up, the visitor backs up out of reach, waits for the puppy to calm down, and tries again. If the guest gets all the way to the puppy and he jumps up when she reaches down, she should quickly back out of reach again. No petting until he doesn't jump up, and if he jumps up during the petting, the guest should once again quickly back out of reach. Repeat this until your guest can walk up to your puppy, pet him, give him a treat, and walk away without him jumping on her.

Leash method: Same as tether method, only you are holding the leash firmly while someone approaches. With the leash you can also work on approaching someone, backing up when the puppy begins to jump. Make sure that no one greets your puppy unless he isn't jumping or pulling toward them.

Each Day: Work on the "Silent Sit-Stay".
Stage 1, for two days: The three factors in the "Stay" command are distance (how far you go from the puppy), duration (how long you stay away) and distractions (what else is going on). This week, work only on the easiest stays, short distance and duration with no distractions.

Next week you will begin to add to the difficulty, but only one factor at a time. From in front of your puppy, ask him to sit, then briefly hold your hand out like a traffic signal. Look at him for a second, then lean forward and give him a treat. Be sure to quickly reach it all the way to him so he doesn't get up to get it. Stand back up straight, and then say, "Free" quietly and move to indicate the puppy can move around now.

Don't make a big deal of the release – you don't want it to be more fun than the stay. Don't be tempted to make it harder yet – build a strong foundation first. Begin to do 3-4 of these stays in a row before releasing your puppy, so that he begins to relax into the stay and doesn't look forward to the release more than the stay.

Do not treat when releasing your puppy. If he gets up while you are reaching the treat toward him, pull it away and start the stay over.

Stage 2, the rest of the week: Begin to add distance into your stay work. At first just take a tiny step back and return quickly to your puppy to reward and release him (pretend you are on a bungee cord and pulled right back). If your puppy gets up when you try to step back, begin by just swaying back a bit and quickly reward him for the stay. Then move a bit more, and reward. Work up to taking a full step back, and then when that is easy for your puppy, begin to take two steps back, then when that is easy, three steps.

Mix up how many steps you are taking once you get to three steps. Your goal for the week is to try to work up to six steps away from your puppy, returning quickly to reward him.

DO NOT TURN YOUR BACK ON THE PUPPY AT THIS STAGE – if you break eye contact your puppy will think you are done with the exercise and almost certainly get up. We will work on breaking eye contact and walking away at a later stage. Begin to do several stays in a row before releasing him, to help him learn to hold his stay longer. After each stay, go back to him, give him a treat (don't touch him or praise him), and calmly do another stay, repeating 3 or 4 times, then release and praise him. Remember not to tell the puppy to "Stay" - he should assume that if he's in a sit or down and you haven't released him, he should stay there.

The key elements of "Stay" training are: 1) if your puppy can't hold it two times in a row, make it easier for a while; 2) release him when you want him to get up, so he learns to wait for you to tell him rather than getting up when he feels like it; and 3) always return to him to give him a treat rather than calling him to you.

Each Day: Do "Nothing In Life Is Free" with your puppy.
Continue waiting for a sit every single time your puppy wants something. Don't ask for it, just wait until he does it and then say, "Yes!" and give him what it is that he is sitting for. By now your puppy should be figuring out that the best way to get things is to sit in front of you. This is one of the most important things you can teach your puppy, so be sure to keep doing it.

Socialization Checklist:

- Did you take him somewhere new this week?
- Did he meet at least two new people this week?
- Did he see at least two new things this week (like umbrellas, people wearing hats, roller skaters)?
- Did he walk on lots of different surfaces this week?
- Did he play with other puppies or friendly dogs this week?

Remember: Keep sessions short and fun!

WEEK THREE

Things to accomplish this week:

- Think about better ways to respond when your puppy does something you don't like
- Start putting "Sit" on a variable reinforcement schedule; i.e. begin to treat for faster sits, not every one
- Improve your puppy's response to "Down"
- Teach the "Watch" command
- Continue to work on the recall
- Keep working on greetings with "four on the floor"
- Adding challenges to the "Silent Stay"
- Work on impulse control - "Leave It", Stage Three
- Continue to work on good leash manners
- Continue to require the "Nothing In Life Is Free" policy – Sit for everything
- Socialization checklist

"Bad Puppy!"

When you catch your puppy misbehaving, it's very tempting to shout "NO!" at him, but the truth is, this rarely helps the situation. Imagine a situation where your puppy is barking uncontrollably, and you start yelling, "NO, QUIET!!!" at him. From his point of view, you are also very excited and barking along with him!

What you really need to do is to interrupt his behavior, and ask him to do something that you do want him to do instead. Use noises to stop any behavior you see that you don't want. Instead of yelling at your puppy, you should make a noise (not scary, just interesting, like a kissy sound or a hand clap), and your puppy will stop what he's doing and look at you. At that moment, you say "Yes!" and give him a treat, or you can simply redirect him to do something you prefer, such as asking him to sit or to play with a chew toy.

So, for the barking example, make your noise, and when you have his attention, ask him to "Sit", then give him the treat. If he's chewing a shoe (shame on you for leaving it lying around!), don't chase him – make your noise and wave a favorite toy for him, and when he leaves the shoe, just casually go and pick it up and put it away. With consistency on your part, he will learn that doing something else works better for him, and you will see a decrease in his unwanted behaviors.

If he isn't near you, you can interrupt by throwing something near him (not AT him), to startle him into paying attention, and then distract him and ask for something else, or replace what he's chewing on with a toy, etc. Whatever you use to get his attention should be enough to make him look up, but not so intense that you scare him.

Remember that the key to a well-mannered puppy is to not allow him to get into the habit of doing something wrong, so the more you avoid the situation, the easier it will be to stop it when it does happen. Train him right away that you don't want him to jump all over people, and you won't need to spend weeks teaching him to stop. Crate train him (see Appendix A if you need help with this) so you have a safe place to keep him when you can't be watching. Think of bad behaviors as potential habits – don't let them form, because they are hard to break!

THINGS TO DO THIS WEEK

Each Day: Practice the "Sit" command using variable reinforcement.

Variable reinforcement is when you stop giving a treat for each time your puppy does the behavior you asked for, and you begin to "vary" the number of behaviors you require before giving a treat. Initially start treating for two or three sits in a row, and then begin to help him learn to get better at it by treating him only for "good" sits – fast ones.

Get an idea of his average sit time, and treat if he does better than that, and not if it's worse or the same. This will teach him to speed up and do quick sits for you. Be sure to remember to release him from each sit – you want him to sit until you say "Free" to get up.

Each Day: Improve your puppy's response to Down".

Practice this each day. As your puppy gets better as responding, you should try not to bend over while asking him, so he doesn't think you always must bend down for him to lie down. Be sure to remember to release him after he does it with "Free". Begin to walk around and then ask for a down, to encourage him to down in any situation.

Each Day: Practice "Watch".

You have already been working on eye contact in your leash manners work, so this should be easy to start for your puppy. Standing in front of him, say "Watch" and when he looks at you, say "Yes!" and treat. Wait until he isn't looking at you and repeat. When he is readily making eye contact with you, begin to make this a bit harder by waiting one second while maintaining eye contact before marking and treating. Over the week, work up to 5 seconds of eye contact at a time, increasing just one second at a time.

Begin to require extra focus by holding out a treat in one hand to the side, out of your puppy's reach. This is actually a form of "Leave It" – the puppy must stop looking at the treat and look back at you in order to get the treat. The instant he looks you in the eye, say "Yes!" and give him the treat that was in your hand. Then start building up more time as above.

Each Day: Continue to play "Recall" games with your puppy.

Continue to work on your puppy's recall. Play games, and call him throughout the day when you are sure he will come to you. The more you do this, the more likely it is that he will come to you when you need it. Remember - practice, practice, practice.

If you have a fenced yard, begin to do this outside. If you don't have a fenced area, you can use a long line (a 15-50 foot leash) to keep him from running off. Keep close together when playing the "Back and Forth Game", and if he wanders off to do something else, try it with better food treats or when he is hungrier.

If he still is too interested in what's in the yard, play more in the house until he loves the game more. Remember to grab your puppy's collar every time before giving him his treat.

Each Day: Practice good greeting behavior.
Continue to work on good greeting behaviors as described in last week's lesson. The more people you work
on this with, the more your puppy learns that going up to
someone means he sits nicely or stands with all feet on
the floor to say hi.

Each Day: Work on the "Silent Stay".
Remember the three factors in the "Stay" command –
distance, duration and distractions. This week, begin to
add mild distance and duration challenges to your puppy's "Stay". Do this one at a time – while you work on
longer stays, stick close to him. When you work on stays
from farther away, don't ask for long stays.

Remember to increase difficulty in small increments –
the biggest mistake most owners make is trying to move
too fast. This is an important exercise, so be sure to create
a strong foundation. If you find he breaks his stay, use a
body block to keep him in place if you can. If not, just put
him back in the same spot and start over. If he cannot
hold the stay you are asking for, you are probably asking
for too much. Make it a bit easier and try again.

Remember to treat during the stay, and release with a
"Free". Don't make the release exciting – you don't want
him to feel that being released is a big fun thing.

Don't forget the key elements of "Stay" training: 1) if your
puppy can't hold it two times in a row, make it easier for a
while; 2) release him every single time, so he learns to
wait for you to tell him to get up rather than getting up
when he feels like it; and 3) always return to him to give
him a treat rather than calling him to you.

Be sure to practice stays with both sits and downs.

Each Day: Practice Impulse Control.
Leave It Game Stage Three: At this point, your puppy should be excellent at leaving a pile of food in your hand or on the floor alone, and waiting for you to give him treats rather than trying to take them. Be sure to keep practicing these steps, but do it in different locations so your puppy understands that it's not just something for the living room, but anywhere.

We will now "up the ante" by adding movement to the treats. This engages the puppy's prey drive, and makes it a real challenge. You should now begin to drop treats near him, place them on his feet, roll them past him, etc. to clinch the lesson that when you say "Leave It", it doesn't matter what it is doing, the puppy should not try to grab it.

Begin to practice with toys or other objects that the puppy is interested in. Make sure the puppy can't grab the treat or toy before you can protect it! Move it a bit farther away from him if necessary.

BE SURE TO ALWAYS SAY "GET IT!" WHENEVER ALLOWING YOUR PUPPY TO PICK SOMETHING UP FROM THE FLOOR OR THIS LESSON WILL NOT BE EFFECTIVE!!!

Each Day: Begin work on "Let's Go".
"Let's Go" is a less formal version of "Heel". Heel means "stay exactly at my left leg, moving with me until I stop, then sit". "Let's Go" means walk with me on my left side, and it's your job to pay some attention to me and not pull on the leash. For strong pullers or tiny dogs, use a front clip harness for leash walking from now on.

This exercise is just like the second part of Exercise 2 from last week, except that we are now using a leash. If your puppy is on your left, you should hold the leash in your right hand and give treats using your left so you won't be reaching across your body with the treat, which may make your puppy try to move in front of you. If the puppy is on your right, you should hold the leash in your left hand and treat with your right.

Keep the leash loose enough that there is a "j" shape hanging down from his collar/harness. If the "j" shape disappears, your puppy is pulling you. You are teaching him that it is his responsibility to keep the leash loose in this lesson.

In a quiet area inside, with your puppy leashed, get your puppy by your side, give him a treat or two, and say "Let's Go" and take a few steps. After a couple of steps, say "Yes!" and give him a great treat. Then take another couple of steps, and if he goes with you, say "Yes!" and give him a treat.

This week, continue walking around with him, saying "Yes!" and giving him a treat, varying from two to ten steps. Just walk around, treating every few steps, getting him used to being next to you, exactly like last week, except this time he is leashed.

Vary your speed and direction so he has to pay attention to what you are doing. You can say "This way" when you change directions to help your pup go along with you. Just do this for a minute or two several times a day. Next week we will begin to make this more challenging.

IF HE PULLS: STOP! Do not let your puppy pull you somewhere ever again! From now on, tension on the leash means he DOESN'T get where he's headed, instead of he does. Wait for him to look back at you (most likely he will be wondering why you aren't following him like you used to), and coax him back by your side (use kissy noises or pat your leg – do not call him), and when he's back in position, say "Let's Go" and take a step or two, and if he doesn't pull, say "Yes!" and give him a treat.

Have patience with this – your puppy has most likely learned to get somewhere by pulling you to it, and he has to learn that the rules have changed now, not to mention that he sees your pace as incredibly slow.

If you walk your puppy on the leash outdoors during the week, even if you do nothing else with this, stop allowing him to pull. The instant the leash gets tight, you stop and wait until he loosens it before you get going again. Be sure to praise and/or treat for loosening up the leash, but don't give him treats until he has walked nicely for a few steps with you, or he will "yo-yo" out to the end of the leash and back to you for a treat.

And don't use a retractable leash, or he won't be able to keep the leash loose.

Each Day: Do "Nothing In Life Is Free" with your puppy.

Continue waiting for a sit every single time your puppy wants something. Don't ask for it, just wait until he does it and then say, "Yes!" and give him what it is that he is sitting for. By now your puppy should be figuring out that the best way to get things is to sit in front of you. This is one of the most important things you can teach your puppy, so be sure to keep doing it.

Socialization Checklist:

- Did you take him somewhere new this week?
- Did he meet at least two new people this week?
- Did he see at least two new things this week (like umbrellas, people wearing hats, roller skaters)?
- Did he walk on lots of different surfaces this week?
- Did he play with other puppies or friendly dogs this week?

Remember: Keep sessions short and fun

WEEK FOUR

Things to accomplish this week:

- Focus on building polite, patient behavior
- Add automatic sits to "four on the floor" greetings
- Improve on leash walking
- Work on impulse control - "Leave It", Stage Four
- Teach "Wait" at doorways
- Teach nose target – Hand Touch
- Add more challenges to the "Silent Stay"
- Continue to work on "Watch"
- Continue to work his name response, "Sit", "Down", "Stay", and "Come" in new locations and situations
- Continue to require the "Nothing In Life Is Free" policy – Sit for everything
- Socialization checklist

What Makes a Good Dog, Anyway?

When most people think of a good dog, they think of a polite dog that sits to greet guests, comes when called, doesn't chew the furniture, isn't pushy, and is attentive and responsive when asked to do something. This is actually asking an awful lot of a dog – they simply don't naturally do these things! Think of them as like a small child – without loving rules and boundaries, they will run amok, at the mercy of their moods and desires. When you establish guidelines that you hold to firmly, they are able to gain control of their impulses and begin to learn to wait patiently for things instead of demanding them, to be attentive to you, and to make appropriate choices about their behavior.

This week we are working hard on teaching your puppy self control and the ability to wait. We will add challenges to his "Stay", look for more self control during greetings, and add a new command that helps him to learn patience and control over his impulses, "Wait". We are working hard on teaching your puppy that mastering his emotions has great rewards, and he is building that "self control muscle" with every training session.

Bear in mind that all of this takes time and practice – your puppy will not suddenly morph into a quiet, polite dog instantly. But you are laying the groundwork and creating new habits and behaviors that will lead to a happy, polite, responsive dog that looks to you for guidance instead of just reacting to everything in sight. Do the work now, and you'll get the rewards the rest of his life!

THINGS TO DO THIS WEEK

Each Day: Begin to notice if your puppy is being rewarded for pushy or rude behavior.
You may not realize it, but you may actually be rewarding your puppy for being pushy. If you have ever reached down to pet him when he nudges you or barks at you, then you have rewarded that behavior. Some of the time you can still pet him, but ask him to sit or lie down first – that way you are rewarding a behavior you want, not the demand. Notice what your puppy does to get your attention, and make sure you are not inadvertently reinforcing rude behavior.

Each Day: Begin to require a sit when your puppy greets someone.
We have been requiring "four on the floor", but now begin to require a sit during a greeting. Say "Sit" as you approach anyone with the puppy on leash. If the puppy approaches but doesn't sit, have the guest wait until he does. Don't say the command again – just have them wait. If the puppy jumps up instead of sitting, back away, and try it from the top. After your puppy does several approaches with a "Sit" command, try it without the command.

We want the puppy to learn to approach someone and sit without prompting. If he doesn't sit, wait a few seconds to give him a chance to figure out what you want. The first time he sits without being asked, give him a jackpot! 5 or more treats in succession and lots of praise! If he doesn't, back up and try again, asking for a sit a few more times, then try without the command again.

Remember that for some puppies, calm greetings are extremely difficult, and it may take a month or more of work to get him to where he can do it, but if you keep trying, he will be able to walk up to a visitor and sit nicely.

Each Day: Work on leash manners.
This week we will continue to walk with your puppy as we learned last week, but now we will add the "Back Away" to your leash work. With your puppy on your left, say "Let's Go" and take a step or two, hesitate and start to back up, coaxing him to turn back toward you with kissy noises and pats on the leg. When he turns his head, say "Yes!" and while continuing to move backward slightly, offer him a treat.

Be sure to hold the treat close to your leg so your puppy must come all the way to you to get it. Then say, "Let's Go", take a couple of steps forward, and do another "Back Away". This week, do "Back Aways" every 2-10 steps of walking both in the house and out.

You are looking for your puppy to do a full 180 turn around toward you. You then treat and keep going forward. At first you may have to take many steps backward drawing him with you, but as your puppy figures out what you want, begin to take fewer steps back. Your goal is for him to see you signal the back away by your hesitation before starting to back up, and to immediately (and reflexively) turn to you.

You can ultimately use this to get him to turn away from things, such as squirrels, other dogs, people, etc. in order to keep him focused or if necessary, to keep him from trying to lunge at them.

Note that we aren't giving a command for this, just hesitating and backing up - you want your puppy to pay attention to what you are doing, without having to nag him. If you are continually unpredictable - changing direction, backing up, changing speed - he will pay more attention to you while walking.

Another important thing to add to your leash work is the "Go Sniff" command. You need your puppy to be able to sniff around and maybe do his business sometimes, but you don't want him sniffing and stopping the whole walk, so you need to have a way to give him permission to stop and check something out.

To teach "Go Sniff", approach something you think will be interesting to your puppy, and if he's not pulling, say "Go Sniff" and run over to the spot with him. Let him check it out for a minute or so, and then say "Let's Go" and start walking again. At first you may have to drag him away from the spot, but be firm. "Let's Go" means walk with me. When he begins to walk nicely again, be sure to reward him.

Having a "Go Sniff" command is great to help allow your dog some freedom on walks (no pulling even when on a sniff break, however), and it helps teach the dog that even the good smells outside are a gift from you, which lets you get a bit more respect from your dog. If you follow these steps when walking your dog, he will learn to look at you for permission to go sniff something instead of trying to drag you to it.

Each Day: Practice Impulse Control.
Leave It Game Stage Four: As we begin to make this game harder again, stand in a doorway for this exercise, since you will be physically blocking your puppy's access

to a treat and it should not be easy for your puppy to get around you. With your puppy in front of you and paying attention, say "Leave It" and toss a treat behind you, stepping aside slightly so that your puppy can see it.

As he makes a move to go get it, block his access with your body. When he gives up trying to get by you, move aside again, and block him again if he tries for it. Be sure to stop him from getting the treat – step on it if necessary. When you can step aside and he doesn't try for the treat, say "Yes!" and give him a different (better) treat from your hand.

Be sure to pick up the treat from the floor – don't let your puppy get it first! Your puppy needs to start understanding that "Leave It" doesn't mean "Wait until I give it to you" - it means "You can't have that". Practice this exercise until you can be sure your puppy won't try to get the treat behind you. Then take a bigger chance and move out of the doorway and do this exercise, being sure you can step on the treat if you can't block your puppy.

Work on this until your puppy will not move towards a dropped treat. Always remember that if you drop something on the floor and he is going to get it because you can't beat him to it, say "Get It!" as if it were your idea. From now on, anytime your puppy gets food from the floor, you should always give him permission to take it by saying "Get It!". Be sure to only say "Leave It" once.

Each Day: Work on "Wait" at doorways.
The difference between "Wait" and "Stay" might seem insignificant, but it is important. Stay asks the puppy to be in a sit or down and hold it until released. Wait means to freeze temporarily. You would use this before going out a door, getting out of the car, or any other time you want

your puppy to hold still. Although you will have your puppy leashed for safety, do not use the leash to hold the puppy. He needs to learn to stop himself, and if you use the leash, you are undermining the lesson in addition to possibly hurting your puppy.

Approach a door with your puppy. At the door, be sure your puppy is a couple of feet back, or use your body to push into him to back him up. Stand by the door, turn partly to your puppy, and say "Wait". Open the door a bit, and be ready to block your puppy as he runs for it. When he hesitates, move aside a bit, and if he doesn't try to rush the door again, say "Free" and let him out. If he does rush at it, just block it again, wait until it looks like he won't run out, and move aside again.

Don't go out until he holds his wait for at least a fraction of a second, and be sure to release him before you both go out. Go back inside and practice again. Do this a couple of times each time you go through a door.

Be sure your puppy is safely leashed during this exercise unless the door you are using opens into a securely fenced yard. In the beginning stages he should be leashed anyway in case he slips through - you want to be able to get him back easily so you can try again.

Each Day: Practice targeting – Hand Touch.
Quickly put your flat hand ¼" away from your puppy's nose, and as he turns toward it, say "Yes!" and give him a treat. Remove your hand, and repeat your motion. If the puppy touches it, say "Yes!" and treat. If not, try again, a bit closer. Be sure to hold your hand in a very different position from how you indicate "Stay".

As he begins to understand that touching your hand earns a treat, begin to say "Touch" before presenting the hand. You don't need to use a verbal command, but it comes in handy if your puppy isn't looking at you.

If he doesn't touch your hand, don't just leave it there - take it away and quickly put it back right in front of his nose.

After he reliably touches your hand from ¼ to ½ inch away, begin to present your hand from a bigger distance, but VERY GRADUALLY. At first an inch, then two inches, etc. Your puppy will probably find it fairly easy to do if he can stretch his neck, but to get him to get up and walk to your hand will require patient work. Remember that if he fails two times in a row, you need to make the exercise easier for him for a while.

This is a great tool for moving your puppy around, getting his attention in a distracting environment, and teaching tricks such as "Spin". Also, since most dogs think "Touch" is great fun once they've learned it, you can use it as a re-call - stick out your hand and say "Touch", and he will run to you to touch your hand!

Each Day: Increase challenges to "Sit/Stay" and "Down/Stay".
Begin to add new challenges to your stays – start turning away when you walk away from your puppy, go out of sight for a second, walk around your puppy, jog past him, bang on a wall, sing, pretend to be talking to someone else. If you have another person who can help, use them to provide additional distractions.

Remember that if your puppy breaks the stay 3 times in a row, you need to make it a bit easier. You goal is for a puppy who can stay no matter what is going on around him.

For a systematic way to increase distractions with little effort on your part, start working through the "Relaxation Protocols", a series of progressive stays by behaviorist Dr. Karen Overall. You can download MP3's of these at

http://www.championofmyheart.com/relaxation-protocol-mp3-files

courtesy of Roxanne Hawn.

Although these are called "days" they are really "steps". Stay on "Day 1" until your puppy can do it without getting up during the exercise, and then move to "Day 2", etc. I prefer to do these with the puppy in a "Down" rather than a "Sit", since it is a more relaxed position. After a bit, you don't need to say "Stay" for each part. Quietly give your puppy a treat after each individual stay, and release at the end of the session.

If your puppy gets up, try to get him back into a down and continue on. If he gets up each time you get to a certain point, work on just that step separately before trying the whole "Day" again. Remember – never reprimand the puppy for a mistake, just help him do better next time.

Don't forget the key elements of "Stay" training: 1) if your puppy can't hold it two times in a row, make it easier for a while; 2) release him every single time, so he learns to wait for you to tell him to get up rather than getting up when he feels like it; and 3) always return to him to give him a treat rather than calling him to you.

Each Day: Work on "Watch".
This week work on stretching out your puppy's ability to maintain eye contact with you. Start requiring longer times – if he is good at 5 seconds of eye contact, try to work up to 10 seconds. See if he can hold eye contact with a mild distraction, like moving your leg a little. If not, begin to work on this, using the same gradual techniques we have used to improve stays and other behaviors.

Also, go outside with this. Since this is a highly distracting environment for most puppies, only ask for the easiest eye contact. You have been getting eye contact while the puppy is on leash for a few weeks now, as part of your leash work. You are now going to ask for eye contact while outside on the leash. Say "Watch", and the instant he looks, say "Yes!" and treat. Then begin to delay the mark and treat by one second at a time until he can hold eye contact outside for 5 or more seconds.

Each Day: Practice name response, "Sit", "Down", "Stay", and "Come" in different locations and situations.
Continue to work on all of the commands your puppy has learned, starting to ask him to do them in slightly more difficult ways. Move your location, have small distractions around, ask for longer stays. Begin to run around and quickly stop and ask for a behavior – this helps your puppy go from an excited state (running after you) to a calm one (sitting or lying down) quickly.

Each Day: Do "Nothing In Life Is Free" with your puppy.
Continue waiting for a sit every single time your puppy wants something. Don't ask for it, just wait until he does

it and then say, "Yes!" and give him what it is that he is sitting for.

Socialization Checklist:

- Did you take him somewhere new this week?
- Did he meet at least two new people this week?
- Did he see at least two new things this week (like umbrellas, people wearing hats, roller skaters)?
- Did he walk on lots of different surfaces this week?
- Did he play with other puppies or friendly dogs this week?

Remember: Keep sessions short and fun!

WEEK FIVE

Things to accomplish this week:

- Pay attention to and reward calm behavior
- Increase the difficulty of the "Down-Stay"
- Practice greetings
- Improve Hand Targeting – Moving "Touch"
- Improve on leash walking
- Work on the "Emergency Down" – fast downs from a distance
- Practice impulse control - "Leave It", Stage Five
- Teach "Go To Your Mat"
- Work on Restrained Recalls
- Continue to work his name response, "Sit", "Down", "Wait", "Watch" and "Come"
- Continue to require the "Nothing In Life Is Free" policy – Sit for everything
- Socialization checklist

What Makes a Good Dog, Anyway? Part 2
As you well know, young dogs have an extraordinary amount of energy, and in order to help them learn self-control, they simply must have enough exercise and mental stimulation to keep from going stir-crazy. If you are making sure he is properly exercised and are working daily on his training, you are helping your puppy to use his energy constructively rather than destructively. Through training, you are teaching him self-control, a critical skill for living with humans.

As we discussed last week, many of our training exercises, such as "Stay", "Wait" and "Leave It" teach self-control. We will continue to build on these behaviors this week (indeed throughout your puppy's lifetime), and also we will begin to focus on calmness in your puppy.

If your puppy is in a feverish state of excitement constantly, he has tons of adrenaline running through his system, and he becomes physically unable to settle down. Liken this to a small child who gets over-tired – he simply can't control himself anymore. In order to prevent this from happening to your puppy, begin to watch for any signs that he is getting over-stimulated and interrupt him for some down time.

Letting him have a timeout in the crate, or giving him a new chew toy (chewing is a stress reliever for dogs) can help an over-excited puppy settle down. To encourage calm behavior, practice switching games constantly – rev him up a bit and then ask for a sit or down.

Also, begin to work on long down-stays. The long down is a great way to teach your puppy to relax and be calm. By spending some time each day working on distractions during a down-stay, you can build up to a dog that will take most things in stride – an easy-going, calm pet.

THINGS TO DO THIS WEEK

Each Day: Begin to notice if your puppy is starting to become over-stimulated.
If you catch your puppy getting too worked up, interrupt him by either giving him a new chewie or by having him spend some down time in the crate. Try to catch him before he gets out of control – you don't want him to make a habit of being wild and crazy.

An exception to this is the "Puppy Zoomies" - a normal phenomenon where puppies run around like crazy once or twice (sometimes more) a day. This is fine - he only might need to be crated or distracted if he gets so excited he starts biting or barking in an out-of-control way.

Each Day: Play "Rev and Relax" games.
Spend time running around and exciting your puppy a bit, and then freeze and ask for a "Sit" or "Down". Be sure to reward heavily for fast responses – you are building your puppy's ability to calm down quickly from stimulating circumstances, something that goes a long way toward having a mannerly pet.

Each Day: Increase the difficulty of the "Down-Stay".
If you've been doing the "Relaxation Protocols" from last week's lesson, you should be systematically increasing your puppy's ability to hold a stay during distractions. Keep on working with this, and also do other distraction work.

While your puppy is in a "Down-Stay", begin to change what you do around him, one change at a time. Take steps to the side, turn away from him slightly, begin to do things like gently clap your hands or lightly tap a wall. See if you can pick up a toy, and work to get him to stay while you roll or gently toss a toy past him.

As the week goes on, increase the level of distractions you are doing, as well as the length of time your puppy can hold the stay.

Don't forget the key elements of "Stay" training: 1) if your puppy can't hold it two times in a row, make it easier for a while; 2) release him every single time, so he learns to wait for you to tell him to get up rather than getting up when he feels like it; and 3) always return to him to give him a treat rather than calling him to you.

Each Day: Continue to work on greetings.
Polite greetings take lots of practice. Take every opportunity you can to work on your puppy sitting before being petted by guests or strangers. Refer back to Week Four for review.

Each Day: Work on "Moving Touch" hand targeting.
If your puppy is confidently moving toward you to touch your hand when you say "Touch" and extend it, you are ready to begin the "Moving Touch". Say "Touch" and extend your hand as usual, but instead of treating when he touches it, take a small step and move your hand with you. As your puppy moves forward to touch your hand again, say "Yes!" and give him a treat. When he confidently follows one step, begin to lead him small distances

by your hand, GRADUALLY increasing the number of steps you ask him to take.

Each Day: Work on leash manners.
Continue to work on leash walking as before, using "Back Aways" constantly. As your puppy gets better, stretch out the number of steps between treats. Be sure not to ask for too much from him if you take him outside on the leash. At first, do your leash work on a paved area such as a driveway, patio or parking lot.

Have several short sessions of "Let's Go" close work alternating with "Back Aways" during a walk outside. It's too difficult for him to do this for a long walk. If you keep it short and fun, he'll look forward to it.

Practice for a short while, then release him and let him walk however he wants as long as he doesn't pull you. When he pulls, YOU MUST STOP or he will never learn that pulling doesn't work. If it works sometimes, he will just try harder next time.

Be sure to reward him whenever he is walking nicely, even if you aren't "training". You want this to become his normal way of walking, so don't take nice work for granted.

If you do a "Back Away" every time your puppy tries to pull toward something, he will begin to turn to look at you each time he sees something interesting instead of running toward it. This could even include squirrels, if you practice enough! The trick here is to catch him at the very beginning of his interest and turn him back. If you wait until he gets focused, it's too late and you will have to drag him, which is not the goal here. Great rewards must follow a good "Back Away" from a hard distraction – make it worth it!

Each Day: Work on the "Emergency Down".

Because a perfect recall takes months or even years to train, you need an easy-to-train, reliable emergency command for times when your puppy is running away from you. The easiest of these is the "Down", since it can be taught to become a reflexive response fairly quickly, and has the advantage of stopping the puppy in his tracks. Imagine a situation where your puppy was across the street – if there was a car coming, you would not want him to come to you, but you don't want him to keep running around either. "Down" is a black-and-white behavior – he is or he isn't, unlike a recall, where he may actually come part of the way back to you and then decide to do something else.

The first step to an emergency down should already be part of your daily training – working on quick responses to the down command. Run away from your puppy and then stop, saying "Down!". After he is down, say "Free!" and run away from him again to repeat the exercise. After several times, reward with a great treat or a game of tug.
As his response to the down command improves, you will need to ask him to do it from a distance. Start with him behind a baby gate or fence, and ask for a down. Then move a couple of feet away from the gate and try again. If he can't do it, move a bit closer and try again. Then begin to increase the distance.

When he can quickly lie down from 20 feet away, start working on distance without a barrier. Have your puppy on a long line or leash, starting only from a few feet, and ask for a "Down". If he moves toward you, take his collar and move him back to where he was and try again. Continue to work on this until you can ask for a down from 20 feet away.

The secret to an emergency command is practice. You must work on this with your puppy every day until he no longer thinks about it. You ask for downs while on walks, in the house, in the yard, on a long line – the more locations and situations you practice, the more likely your puppy will respond without thought.

Note that all of this takes time and practice - you will NOT accomplish this in a week. Work on it one step at a time until your dog will drop anytime you say "Down". This could save his life!

BE SURE TO ALWAYS REMEMBER TO RELEASE HIM. THIS IS A DOWN-STAY – HE SHOULD UNDERSTAND TO STAY PUT UNTIL YOU EITHER ASK FOR SOME OTHER BEHAVIOR (E.G. COME), OR YOU RELEASE HIM.

Each Day: Practice Impulse Control.

Leave It Game Stage Five: At this point, your puppy should be easily dealing with Stages One and Two of "Leave It", in your hand and a pile on the floor. He should be able to resist food and toys moving near him, Stage Three, and resist trying to get a piece of food dropped behind you in a doorway, Stage Four.

Now you should begin to use the "Leave It" command about other objects while on leash. Take leash walks in the house, with objects set up for you to walk past. As you approach the object, say "Leave It" and when your puppy looks at you, say "Yes!" and hustle past the object, and then give him a great treat. Don't stay and let him stare at it after he has looked away. If he stares/pulls and won't look at you, WAIT. Don't try to make him look at you with movements or sounds, just hold him firmly where he is. Eventually he will look away from the object in frustration - at THAT INSTANT you must say "Yes!" and move with him quickly away from the object and give him a treat. Next time walk past the object from a greater distance to make it easier for him to look away.

Key points: don't repeat the command, don't try to distract the puppy away from the object, move away from it quickly once he has looked away from it, and do it from farther away if he is having trouble letting it go. You must allow him to make the decision to look away - it is that instant that you must mark his good choice with a "Yes!" and then move quickly away and treat him.

When your puppy is easily leaving objects, start working again with food. Prepare a couple of plates with kibble, and have extra good treats on you (cheese or meat, preferably). While the puppy can't get to the area, put the plates of kibble out where you can walk him past with enough room to keep away from them. Then put your puppy on leash, get his attention, say "Let's Go!" and begin to walk. As you approach a dish, say "Leave It". If he pulls toward it, be sure to not let him get it. Don't yank him back, just keep him firmly away from it. The moment he looks back at you, say "Yes!", quickly walk past the plate, and then give him a treat. Do the same at the next plate.

Continue to work this week so that your puppy will begin to keep walking and look at you for a treat when he sees your "traps". Be sure he never gets it without permission or you will be teaching the wrong lesson! If you work on this, you'll be able to use this for goose poops, chewing gum, trash, and anything else you see on your walks that

114

you don't want your puppy to pick up. Be sure to have great treats so that he realizes that leaving something means he'll get something better. Eventually it will just become a habit to respond to you.

You can also use "Leave It" to draw his attention away from other dogs, people, squirrels, etc.

Each Day: Practice "Go To Your Mat".
To teach this, have tasty treats handy. In a quiet room, put your training mat on the floor a foot or so away from you, say "Go To Your Mat" (or just "Mat" or whatever you prefer), make a swooping motion toward the mat while letting a treat drop on it from the hand that's swooping. When your puppy goes to the mat to get the treat, say "Yes!" and give him another when he's on the mat. To get him off the mat to try again, say "Free", toss a treat a few feet away and say "Get It". Then say "Go to Your Mat" and swoop another treat onto the mat, reward and get him off again.

Repeat this a few times, and then do exactly the same thing only don't toss the treat while swooping your hand toward the mat. If your puppy goes to the mat to look for the treat, then say "Yes!" and give him a jackpot of three or four treats in a row before getting him off to do it again.

Get rid of the "lure" treat as soon as possible – you want him to follow your hand, not a treat, except in the beginning to give him the idea of what you want.

Continue to practice this until he is responding quickly and easily to your request. As he gets better, make sure you insist that all four feet be on the mat, and eventually that he lies down, which is your ultimate goal.

Each Day: Play Recall Games.
To add enthusiasm to your recalls, you will now add two more exercises to your daily recall sessions.

1) If you have a training partner, one of you holds the puppy around the chest and belly while the other revs him up a bit ("Ready, ready..."). Then the "revver" calls the puppy and runs away as the "holder" lets go. The puppy should spring away toward the running person who rewards his arrival with a great treat or, better, a good game of "Tug".

2) Place the puppy in a "Sit". Move a few feet away and rev him up as above. If he breaks the stay, just put him back and try again. Then call him and run as above.
Start with the runner close to the puppy, and gradually increase the head-start you have. Be sure to have a party when the puppy arrives.

Each Day: Practice name response, "Sit", "Down", "Stay", "Watch", "Come", "Touch" and "Wait".
Continue to work on all of the commands your puppy has learned, starting to ask him to do them in slightly more difficult ways. Move your location, have small distractions around, ask for longer stays – make small changes at a time, but keep stretching your puppy's ability to perform. Just remember that if he fails, back up a step. Your goal is to have your puppy be able to succeed – otherwise he isn't learning anything.

Each Day: Do "Nothing In Life Is Free" with your puppy.
Continue waiting for a sit every single time your puppy

wants something. Don't ask for it, just wait until he does it and then say, "Yes!" and give him what it is that he is sitting for.

Socialization Checklist:

- Did you take him somewhere new this week?
- Did he meet at least two new people this week?
- Did he see at least two new things this week (like umbrellas, people wearing hats, roller skaters)?
- Did he walk on lots of different surfaces this week?
- Did he play with other puppies or friendly dogs this week?

Remember: Keep sessions short and fun!

WEEK SIX

Things to accomplish this week:

- Continue to challenge the "Down-Stay"
- Practice greetings
- Improve on leash walking
- Work on impulse control - "Leave It", Stage Six
- Teach the "Take It" and "Drop It" commands
- Continue to work his name response, "Sit", "Down", "Touch", "Watch", "Wait", "Go To Mat" and "Come"
- Continue to require the "Nothing In Life Is Free" policy – Sit for everything
- Socialization checklist

Are We There Yet?

Yes, you are at the end of this six week program, but no, you are not "there yet" in the sense that your puppy still has a ways to go before you can say that he is fully trained. Exactly what that means is really up to you – for some people, a dog who is polite and not a pest or destructive is a well-trained pet, and for others, that means a dog that instantly stops whatever he's doing and jumps to obey any command. Clearly, these are quite different goals and require very different levels of commitment to the training process. You and you alone will decide how far you want to take the training of your puppy.

Even if you don't need your puppy to be a "super dog", you must continue practicing what you have learned here. Puppy training is a "Use it or lose it" proposition, and if you stop all work, your puppy will soon begin reverting back to his former behaviors.

It doesn't take much to integrate training into your day – just remember to ask for things he knows intermittently throughout your time with him. The "Nothing in Life Is Free" policy should be a lifelong habit for you, and it presents you with many opportunities to train your puppy throughout your day. Use these times to practice quick responses to "Sit" and "Down". While watching TV, ask your puppy for a "Down-Stay", and toss him a treat now and then while he's doing it. Practice "Leave It" before giving him a treat or new toy, play a quick game of "Chase Me" before giving him his supper.

Remember, especially for a recall, practice should be often and fun. Don't expect your puppy will perform at a level you haven't trained for, so if you want better performance, keep working. If you incorporate these requests into your routine, your puppy will continue on his way to becoming a great pet!

THINGS TO DO FROM NOW ON:

Practice "Rev and Relax" games.
Spend time running around and exciting your puppy a bit, and then freeze and ask for a "Sit" or "Down". Be sure to reward heavily for fast responses – you are building your puppy's ability to calm down quickly from stimulating circumstances, something that goes a long way toward having a mannerly pet.

Work on the "Down-Stay".
This is a critical exercise in self-control, and the more challenges your puppy can handle, the less reactive he is to things in the environment. Try to work up to 30 minutes during the evening while you are watching TV. Work on your puppy staying during distractions like the doorbell, a whistle being blown, you running past him, you leaving the room, someone else walking past him – pretty much anything you can think of. Doing the Relaxation Protocol exercises can help with this.

If you can get your puppy to think that everything that is happening is a trick to get him up, and no, he's not going to fall for it, then you have done a fine job! Just remember – progress slowly enough that he can handle whatever it is you are doing. Stretch his abilities a little at a time, and soon he will be able to lie down calmly for almost anything.

Continue to work on greetings.
Polite greetings take lots of practice. Take every opportunity you can to work on your puppy sitting before being petted by guests or strangers. Refer back to Week Four for review.

Each Day: Work on leash manners.
Great leash walking takes time and practice. Continue to work on leash walking as before, using "Back Aways" constantly. Use a "Back Away" every time your puppy begins to lock onto something during your leash walking work – you want him to easily let go of it and turn to you. Remember, if you do this diligently, he will begin to turn to look at you each time he sees something interesting instead of running towards it.

ALWAYS HAVE TREATS DURING A WALK!!! You can also begin to use a "Go Sniff" as a reward for good walking, which might be a better reward than treats.

While on walks, be sure to stop regularly and ask your puppy for something – sit, down, touch, etc. Change directions and pace frequently – walk slowly and then start to jog for a few steps. The more you vary what you do on a walk, the more interesting you are to your puppy, and the more he will pay attention to you. Walks should be about being together, not just your puppy sniffing everything around him.

Practice Impulse Control.
Leave It Game Stage Six: This week, you will continue to test your puppy's ability to resist in "real-life" situations, putting food on furniture and counters (if your puppy is tall enough to counter-surf). Put your puppy on leash. Place a dish of relatively uninteresting food, such as kibble, on a plate, and place the plate on a chair or low table. With you between the puppy and the food, walk past it, and if your puppy doesn't pay much attention, give him a treat that is better than what's on the plate.

Work up to being able to walk the puppy by when the food is on his side, just be sure you have control over him so he can't take it. By now you should have reinforced him heavily with extra great treats for not trying to get things, so this should be pretty easy for him.

REMEMBER TO ALWAYS SAY "GET IT" WHEN GIVING A TREAT THAT IS ON THE FLOOR TO HELP YOUR PUPPY KNOW HE CAN TAKE IT!

Teach the "Take It" and "Drop It" commands.

Take It: Hold an enticing tug toy out of reach of your puppy. Wait for him to sit without you asking, and then say "Take It" and let him grab the toy. After a short game of tug, ask for a "Drop It" as described below.

As your puppy begins to understand that he is not to grab things out of your hand, but to sit and wait for the command, begin to test him. Move the toy in reach, and if he grabs/jumps at it, quickly pull it up and away, wait for him to sit, and try again.

If you need to, make it easier for your puppy to succeed by holding the toy farther away again, and work back to closer. Eventually you should be able to touch him with the toy and he won't grab it until told he can.

Drop It: While the puppy has something in his mouth, say "Drop It" and then hold a smelly treat right against his nose. When he drops the object to get the treat, say "Yes!" and give him the treat while taking the object out of reach. You should do this with something the puppy is readily willing to let go of at first, and then work up to harder things as he gains the understanding of what you mean. Be sure to always start a game of tug with "Take It" and end it with "Drop It".

Do this tug sequence several times a day, and he will begin to willingly drop his toy for you. After he starts dropping the toy quickly when asked while the treat is near his nose, try asking without presenting the treat. If he even loosens his grip on the toy, whip out the treat and give it to him, and then do a "Take It" and play a bit. If not, just put the treat by his nose, work for a few more days on it and try again.

This is a wonderful behavior that you'll use often over his lifetime – to drop goose poops, dead mice, candy wrappers, your kid's toys, slippers, and the like. Just don't make the mistake of thinking that your puppy will drop something special like deer poop until you have totally trained this on harder and harder items.

This behavior is just like any other – you must work up to the challenges, so don't bother to ask for a drop if you know he won't do it. Simply wave a great treat in front of his nose to exchange the item, and treat it as if you are training the "Drop It".

Practice name response, "Sit", "Down", "Stay", "Touch", "Watch", "Go To Mat", "Emergency Down", "Come" and "Wait".
Practice the commands you have taught your puppy as part of your daily routine, or he will forget them. The more they matter to you, the more you must work to increase his proficiency. A great recall usually takes months, and sometimes years to perfect – and that's working on it every day.

Too many times people expect that because a puppy can come in the house or backyard when nothing is going on, they should be able to come back when chasing a squirrel.

This will not happen without consistent, progressive work on your part.

And please, don't risk your puppy's life on a recall that you know isn't perfect. Always keep him on a leash or in a securely fenced area when he is outside. Once your puppy becomes attentive to you outside, you can have him drag a "long line", or 15-50 foot leash that gives you a way of grabbing him if he starts to run off. Be sure he can't reach a street or other dangerous area before you can catch him though.

Do "Nothing In Life Is Free" with your puppy.
Continue waiting for a sit every single time your puppy wants something. Don't ask for it, just wait until he does it and then say, "Yes!" and give him what it is that he is sitting for.

Socialization Checklist:

- Did you take him somewhere new this week?
- Did he meet at least two new people this week?
- Did he see at least two new things this week (like umbrellas, people wearing hats, roller skaters)?
- Did he walk on lots of different surfaces this week?
- Did he play with other puppies or friendly dogs this week?

Remember: Keep sessions short and fun!

A NOTE ON REWARDS

As your puppy has become better at what you've been teaching, you should have already begun to only give treats for better performances, such as fast sits and downs, longer stretches of good leash walking, etc. As you move ahead with practice of known behaviors, be sure to vary when your puppy gets a reward, and also begin to use more "real-life rewards" in your training. This should be what you've been doing with the "Nothing in Life Is Free" training, but you should begin to use this more and more for training rewards.

Get a solid "Down-Stay" before you throw the Frisbee, take a tug toy with you on a walk and stop and play for a minute after some excellent leash work, call your puppy to you and reward with a game of fetch – just be sure that whatever you're using is something of high value to your puppy. If your puppy hates fetch, don't use that – it's not a reward. It helps to make a list of all of the things your puppy really loves, and then use those as rewards.

Continue to use food treats occasionally (it's like a paycheck for your puppy – would you work for long without one?), especially if you are training something new or particularly difficult, but for things he's pretty good at, use lots of other types of rewards. Our goal is to have a willing partner in training, but not one that will only work for food.

IN CLOSING

FREE BONUS! Be sure to go to

www.ReallySimpleDogTraining.com/PTBonus.html

to get your FREE printable quick reference sheet. This lets you print any or all of the instructions for each week so that you don't have to refer to your book while training.

Congratulations on seeing your puppy's training through this far! You are ahead of 99% of the population on making sure you have a great pet for life. Keep up the good work, and remember, puppy training is "use it or lose it", so you want to make sure you practice everything you've taught your puppy or he will begin to forget.

I wish you the best in your efforts to train your puppy. If you diligently follow the steps outlined above, you should see positive results quickly. Just remember that you are teaching your puppy a new way to live, and that this takes time. Patience and a sense of humor are your best tools!

If you enjoyed this booklet, I invite you to write a short review on Amazon to help others find success in their training endeavors. Also I recommend checking out my booklet, "Housetraining Success Formula: 6 Simple Steps to Housetraining Your Puppy or Dog" for Amazon Kindle. If you feel you are ready for more intensive training with your puppy, be sure to take a look at "COME HERE! Teach Your Dog To Come When You Call". This is advanced training in recalling, leash walking, "Leave It" work, and teaches an "Emergency Down". These are skills that can save your dog's life!

Be sure to look for my upcoming booklets in the series "Really Simple Dog Training", coming soon!

Carol Miller, CDT

www.ReallySimpleDogTraining.com

APPENDIX A - Crate Training Your Puppy

One of the most valuable management tools available to dog owners is a crate. While overuse of the crate is definitely bad for your dog, proper crating of your dog or puppy can help manage housetraining, chewing, pesty behaviors like jumping on guests and begging at meals, and can give your dog a safe den to chill out. Many dogs love their crates, but it's not for all dogs. Some, especially those that have been caged or over-crated in the past, may have developed a fear of being confined, and panic in a crate. If this is severe, crating is not an option for the dog. But for most, a crate can be a happy, comfortable place once you've done a little training to get them to associate it with good stuff.

Be sure to choose the correct size for your dog. He should be able to stand up, lie down, and turn around in it, without much extra space. Crates are available in soft sided, plastic (airline-style), and wire. Soft crates are not appropriate for serious chewers. Some wire crates are available with an adjustable wall that lets you fit the same crate correctly as your dog grows. This is very useful for a large breed, which would otherwise need to be refitted several times with a larger crate. You can purchase a mat to fit inside, but if your dog chews beds, you may want to try an old towel and see how it goes first.

Place the crate in an area where your family spends a lot of time, so the dog doesn't feel isolated from everyone while he's crated. He should eventually be able to lie quietly in his crate even when people are in the room.

The Training Process

Be sure your dog doesn't need a potty break. To start, throw some treats around the outside of the crate, and make sure you put a few extra good ones inside it near the door. He will stick his head in to get the treats, and if he's adventurous, may even go all the way inside. DO NOT CLOSE THE DOOR AT THIS POINT! When he comes out, throw more treats inside, a little farther back this time. Once you've gotten to where the dog stands calmly inside eating his treats (this may not happen in your first several training sessions, depending on the dog's history), close the door and quickly reopen it.

Do this a few times until the dog is used to it. Then close it and feed the dog a couple of treats through the door and reopen it. Gradually increase the time you keep the door closed. Don't rush this – you want the dog to learn to like being inside, so increase the time slowly.

Continue increasing the time in the crate, treating often, until he is comfortable remaining inside for 15 minutes or so, while you stay near the crate. Next, begin to step away from the crate for a few seconds at a time, then return to treat through the door and step away again. Gradually increase the time you are away. Then do the same stepping out of sight, coming back to treat him at gradually longer intervals.

If your puppy barks, since you are sure that he doesn't need to go potty, *DO NOT LET HIM OUT OR GIVE HIM A TREAT UNTIL HE STOPS BARKING*. Don't even look at him. If he is insistently barking, wait until he is quiet for a second or two, and quickly say "GOOD!" and drop him a treat. He must learn that barking does NOT get him out of the crate. If you give in, it will only be harder to stop next time, so DON'T!!! Only let him out when he is quiet, even if it is only a few seconds.

You may want to give him a stuffed Kong® toy or a Nylabone® to chew on inside – something that will be safe for him to chew unattended. This can help him occupy himself when he isn't napping, and if the crate is the only place he gets that stuffed Kong®, he may run to go into it without even being told.

You can also increase the appeal of being inside by locking a favorite toy, smelly Kong® or other treat (meat works well for this) inside with your dog outside. Let him spend some time trying to get to the treat before opening the door to let him run in to get it. Play crate games like "chase the treats into the crate" to keep going into the crate fun. Don't only lock him in for long periods of time, or he will stop wanting to go in. It is good practice to give some kind of treat EVERY TIME he goes into the crate to stay for a while.

It is very important not to use the crate as a punishment. You want the crate to be a good, safe place for your dog, not something only used when he is bad. That said, you may find a short time-out in the crate can help settle an over-excited dog or puppy at times. Just be sure when you put him in, you are not reprimanding him. Just get him to go in the crate as usual, and give him a treat or chew toy and let him settle for a few minutes. When trained correctly, a stay in the crate will have a calming effect on the dog, letting him just relax for a while.

WARNING: Be sure not to abuse this tool – a dog crated all day while his owner is at work and all night, with just a couple of hours out in the evening and a short walk in the morning is a neglected animal, and will suffer physically and mentally. If you can't be home during the day and must confine your dog, arrange for someone to come in during the day and give him a bathroom and exercise break or two, or consider doggy daycare. It simply isn't right to keep a dog in a tiny area for the entire day. And remember, puppies and small dogs must have a potty break at regular intervals, as little as 2-4 hours, depending on the dog.

APPENDIX B - Some Common Problem Behaviors in Puppies

Jumping on people. We address this with the "Polite Greeting" exercises in the program. You should be using this when people come home if possible, and definitely if you have children. Work on your kids being able to run up to your puppy without him jumping by using the "Leash" technique in the "Greetings" lessons described above. If you are by yourself and you have no way to hold the dog back from jumping on you, quickly pop into another room and close the door on the dog. Wait a few seconds, come out, and if he jumps, again quickly disappear. Soon he will figure out that if he wants you to stay with him, he must stop jumping on you. Don't say anything - let him see the connection himself: jump and she leaves, don't jump and she stays.

Play biting/nipping. The "Collar Grab" is a great exercise to help with this. Also, don't ever use your hands around the dog like it's a game. For serious play biters, you should work on a variation of the "Collar Grab" where you hold a treat in one hand and let the puppy nibble on it while you touch him on the face and head with the other hand. Work up to touching his face without the nibbling and mark and reward him for not nipping at it. Once you can touch him all over his face and head, start working on the rest of his body.

You want to get him to feel that reaching around any part of him is just no big deal, in fact, he probably will get a treat for it! But not if he bites at your hand. For ankle biting, the best thing to do is to freeze the instant he starts, and not move until he stops. Most of the time people tend to scream and run when this happens (those baby teeth really hurt!), but that just encourages your puppy to think that it's a fun game. Don't be a giant squeaky toy! Sometimes kids can't stand still, so give them treats to keep in their pockets, and when the puppy runs at them have them throw treats on the ground BEFORE he starts nipping. Soon he will be ready to search the ground when he runs to them instead of thinking about their ankles. It's all about replacing the bad habit with a new better one.

Leash biting. Totally ignore this one. When you start working on leash attention in Lesson Two, you should find this dropping off. The less you react to something you don't like, the better, since scolding and struggling seem like a good game to your puppy. Be boring and totally ignore this unwanted behavior. It will go away.

Attention-seeking behaviors. These might be barking at you, grabbing your clothes, nipping at you, jumping on you, and any of a number of obnoxious behaviors. You can tell the difference between regular play biting and biting for attention by when your puppy does it. If he does it while you are doing things with him like petting or playing a game, it's play biting. If he bites you whenever you watch TV or talk on the phone, it's attention-seeking. The best way to deal with attention-seeking behaviors is to not give them any attention. If it gets too difficult to ignore, give the puppy a time-out (calmly, no scolding please), wait a couple of minutes, and if he's quiet, let him out again. Let him learn that there is a connection between his obnoxious behaviors and having to have a time-out.

Clothes grabbing. In Lesson Six, you work on "Take It" and "Drop It". If you have a problem with your puppy grabbing your clothes, you should move that up to the very beginning. Start with your puppy learning not to grab a toy, by practicing "Take It". Do this often, so he starts to really get that he shouldn't grab the toy without permission. Then start working with other things, like an old dish towel. With this, you shouldn't say "Take It" - when he doesn't grab at it even when it's in reach, say "Yes!" and give him a treat. Get to the point where you can touch him with the towel and he doesn't bite at it. Then try other dangly things. This should help dramatically to stop clothes grabbing.

Stealing things and running off with them. First of all, you need to practice better management - he shouldn't have much opportunity for this until you have trained him to listen better. The "Leave It" exercises will help with this, and a good "Drop It" can help get things back. Don't chase him - do something interesting so he drops the object and comes over to see what you're doing, then go take the object and move it out of reach. You simply have to prevent this from happening as much as possible, or he will develop a tough habit to break.

Chewing on your stuff. This also comes back to management. Are you limiting where he can go while he's not being confined in his crate/area? If so, are you watching him like a hawk? Does he have plenty of interesting chewies available? You must make sure he likes them, or it won't do any good. If you see him going over to chew something inappropriate, distract him with a noise (kissy noise or a clap of your hands), and give him one of his own chew toys. Praise him when you see him chewing on his own toys. If you are diligent about this, he will quickly build a habit of thinking of his own toys when he gets the urge to chew. An important note: do not give your puppy old socks, shoes or even stuffed animals as toys if you expect him to keep from chewing your good ones. It's just not fair to ask a dog to figure out when such a similar object to the one you gave him to play with is off limits.

Housetraining Issues. Housetraining is beyond the scope of this book. I recommend my booklet for Kindle titled "Housetraining Success Formula: 6 Simple Steps to Housetraining Your Puppy or Dog" for more information on this topic.

SUMMARY

Most behavior problems can be handled by good management, and this includes training games and plenty of exercise. For the average dog, a walk around the block is a warm-up, not exercise. He needs to run. If you don't have a fenced yard, this can be a challenge.

For small breeds and puppies, chasing a ball around the house will work. If you have stairs, running your dog up and down is great exercise. For larger dogs, you may have to take him daily to the dog park (once he's old enough, and only if he behaves well around other dogs), or do what I have done - go to a local field and tie a 50 foot long line around your waist and throw balls or other toys so your dog can get a good workout. Just be very careful not to trip on the rope!

An excellent trainer once put it to me like this: that energy is going to come out somehow. For a dog it comes out in one of three ways: his feet, his head, or his mouth. It's up to you to channel it properly through exercise and brain work.

APPENDIX C - GLOSSARY

Clicker Training: A method of training new behaviors using a clicker (a small noise maker) to mark the exact behavior that you are rewarding him for. This is used to help a puppy understand what you want from him, and is not needed once he is responding well to your request.

Distractions: Things that may make your puppy lose focus or decide not to obey you. When first teaching any behavior, you should make sure there are no distractions around. This includes other people, noises, interesting smells, toys nearby, commotion in the vicinity, etc. Once your puppy is reliably obeying without distractions, then you begin "proofing", or carefully adding distractions to teach your puppy that he can still listen when something else is around.

Environmental Reinforcers: Things that reward the puppy that don't involve you, such as barking at other dogs, chasing squirrels, eating out of the garbage can, etc.

High value treats: Super special treats that your puppy loves best, which may include real meat, cheese, and dried liver. From some dogs a high value treat would be an ice cube, while others could care less. Your puppy decides the value. Someone can try to convince me that coconut is delicious, but since I hate it, it's not a high value treat for me.

Low value treats: Something your puppy likes enough to work for in a quiet environment, but is too ordinary or not tasty enough that he cares about it when things get harder, such as going outside in the yard. These treats may include the puppy's regular dry food kibbles.

Jackpot: A special reward of 3 to 4 treats giving quickly one after another (the same number of treats in a handful is just one bite, so spread them out), in order to let your puppy know that he has done something great! Times to use this would include the first time he does something correctly, when he has ignored a particularly difficult distraction, or just to surprise him and keep it fun.

Marker Training: Same as clicker training, only we use a word, such as "Yes!" to mark the correct behavior. Clicker trainers still use a marker word sometimes, since they may not always have a clicker on them. This is generally not quite as effective as a clicker, since your word can sound different each time, but is usually fine.

M/T: Mark (click or say "Yes!") and give the puppy a treat.

Positive Reinforcement Training: Training which uses the scientific laws of learning by focusing on rewarding behaviors that you like and want to see again, and by ignoring or replacing behaviors that you don't like and want to eliminate. By using treats, games, and "real life" rewards we can influence how a puppy behaves, and build new habits.

Proofing: The process of systematically working with your puppy through more and more difficult distractions in order to be sure he can respond correctly no matter what is going on around him. Proofing should be done by carefully adding one distraction at a time, and working with that until your puppy is able to ignore it, then moving on. Eventually you should be training around multiple distractions at the same time, but you must work up to this, or your puppy will not be able to succeed.

Real life rewards: Using things the dog wants as his reward for doing what you've asked. Examples would be letting the dog out to play after he sits nicely and waits for you to open the door and release him, or playing tug when he comes when called. The more of this kind of reinforcement you can use with your puppy, the more reliable he will become, since these often are more important to the puppy than treats.

Reinforcer: Rewards, such as food, games, going outside, getting in a car, taking a walk, belly rubs – anything a puppy likes enough to be willing to do things for. Also called a motivator. Be sure the puppy likes it – it's not a reinforcer if he doesn't care about it, even if you think it should be.

Reward: Reinforcer.

Setting the puppy up for success: When training, be sure that you don't move too fast for your puppy, or he won't be able to be correct. When this happens often, he isn't getting enough feedback to know what you actually want from him, since you can't reward him, and you run the risk of frustrating him. Step back and make it easier until he can reliably be correct, and then make the situation just a bit harder for him. If he can't focus on training, ask for something really easy, reward him, and stop for the time being. If you feel yourself getting frustrated, back up, get a good response to reward, and stop. Training should be fun for both of you – if it's not that day, just stop and try later.

Socialization: The process of getting your puppy exposed to new things, especially important early on, in order to avoid him developing fears. Socialization involves having your puppy meet lots of people, other puppies and friendly dogs, going to new places, walking on all types of surfaces (shiny floors, gravel, sidewalks, soft surfaces, wobbly surfaces, etc.), walking near bicyclers, skateboarders, motorcyclists, walking in towns and the woods, visiting the vet's office just to say "hi", rides in the car, etc. You can purchase CD's with scary noises like fireworks, thunder, baby cries and motorcycles and play them at low levels to help your puppy get used to them.

Variable reinforcement schedule: Not giving your puppy treat rewards every time he does what you ask. As your puppy's understanding of what you want from him grows, you must stop rewarding him every single time he responds correctly, or he will begin to think he should always get a treat. Start treating for better responses only, or every second or third time he does it. Always praise, however.

Claim Your Free Bonus

FREE BONUS!

Be sure to go to

www.ReallySimpleDogTraining.com/PTBonus.html

to get your FREE printable quick reference sheet. This lets you print any or all of the instructions for each week so that you don't have to refer to your book while training.

Also be sure to print out your worksheets from Week One.

About the Author

Carol Miller is a Certified Dog Trainer, and an honors graduate of the Animal Behavior College. In addition to her series of dog training books (Really Simple Dog Training), she has written several children's books about nature and the world we live in.

She lives in New Jersey with her family, which includes two rescued Border Collies and 3 rescued cats.

Learn more about "Really Simple Dog Training" at

www.ReallySimpleDogTraining.com

Made in the USA
Middletown, DE
22 May 2016